Notes from Myself

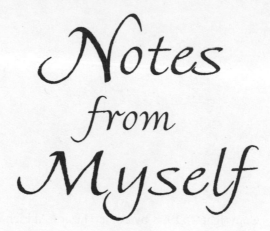

Notes
from
Myself

—

A
Guide to
Creative
Journal Writing

—

Anne
Hazard Aldrich

Illustrations by Hazard Durfee

CARROLL & GRAF PUBLISHERS, INC.
NEW YORK

First Carroll & Graf edition 1998

Carroll & Graf Publishers, Inc.
19 West 21st St., Suite 601
New York, NY 10010-6805

Library of Congress Cataloging-in-Publication Data

Aldrich, Anne Hazard.
Notes from myself : a guide to creative journal writing /
 by Anne Hazard Aldrich.
 p. cm.
Included bibliographical references (p.   ).
ISBN 0-7867-0433-0 (trade paper)
1. Diaries—authorship. 2. Diaries—Therapeutic use. 3. Diaries—
Authorship—Psychological aspects. 4. Creative writing.
I. Title.
PN4390.A53   1998
808'.06692—DC21   97-6786
                                                             CIP

PN
4390
.A53
1998

Manufactured in the United States of America

Contents

Acknowledgments

This book has been a lifetime in the writing. Many lives have touched, intersected with and formed my own life, and many people have entered the pages of my journals. I cannot begin to cover all the thanks and graditude I owe to friends and teachers and all the loved and not so loved ones who have been heroes and villains in the pages of my journal and who have helped create who I am.

So I will start this official thanks from the time I first seriously thought about publishing my writing. My debt to Professor Lawrence Grebstein is not only, as the dedication indicates, for showing me the "Thou" inside, but for encouraging me to take my journal writing seriously. He listened and advised and always sent me home to write. It took.

Mr. Truman MacDonald Tally and the late Madelon Tally were the first professional, 'in the business,' friends to read my work, like it and offer valuable advice and encouragement. They helped plant the germ of becoming a 'writer' in my conscious mind. I am sure, subconsciously, it has lurked there since day one of my life.

Professor Walter Barker inspired a great surge of Shakespeare and Dante papers and encouraged what he felt was a talent for writing.

My sister Jane has read versions of this book from the first typo filled pages and been a wonderful sounding board, as has Mrs. Martina Sasnett, a much admired and loved relative in Santa Barbara.

This book might never have seen the light of publication without the great help and support of my friends Jorge Castello and George Caldwell, owners of Book Hampton in East Hampton. They read the MS when it was still just a dream, and they were instrumental in getting it into the hands of Kent Carroll.

Sondra Winenga has been invaluable as a friend and typist, taking my medieval mess of typewritten pages and producing a superb 21st century rendition which made the book possible to read. She allowed me to stay in my 14th century mind-set while she dealt with contemporary realities.

My uncle Hazard Durfee produced the four inset drawings from a list of quotations I sent him without any guidelines or instructions as to what I wanted. They arrived exactly as I had in mind but could never have explained, a perfect act of *his* creative imagination and a perfect accompaniment to this book. For which I thank him deeply.

Much of this book came into being through chance 'acts of grace,' from moments which seemed to 'click,' and from people who responded to me with just what I needed at the time. It is a book which, in many ways, created itself and, in the writing, has taken on a life of its own. As its author it has been exciting to see what came next in the ongoing mystery which is discovery of hidden creative recesses that winged in from regions unknown. That it was all there, the whole fabric already woven and ready to cut and stitch, I would not have known if I had not started the writing of it.

To Larry—who showed me there is a THOU inside.

"The Thou encounters me by grace—it cannot be found by seeking. But that I speak the basic word to it is a deed of my whole being, is my essential deed."

Martin Buber, *I and Thou*

"Herureux qui, comme Ulysse, a fait un beau voyage..."

Joachim du Bellay, "Sonnet V"

"When you start on your journey to Ithaca,
Then you pray that the road is long,
Full of adventure, full of knowledge...
Ithaca has given you the beautiful voyage.
Without her you would never have taken the road...
With the great wisdom you have gained, with so much
  experience,
You must surely have understood by then what Ithaca means."

C.P. Cafavy, "Ithaca"

Preface

Within each person there exist two lives attempting to cohabitate in peace and pleasure with each other. We are the event-enmeshed person of everyday actions, and we are the inner still self. We move to two tempos: the daily beat of what we must put into each twenty-four hour span, and the unended music of our forever self. The two lives and two tempos cannot be separated without splitting the whole with disastrous consequences. We need to be of a piece.

In this age of dichotomies that separate us into two halves, what was once taken for granted, integrity of personality, is now something we have to work for. It is easy to get caught in a soul stifling prison. But there is an escape if we are willing to use it, if we are open to look for it.

The escape lies in creativity, in our own spirit and instinct. Every human being is born with this instinct; it is what makes us who we are. Sometimes we become so entangled in the mundane facts of our lives that we forget about our creative nature until it starts nagging us with reminders of its needs or until we feel so fractured we know something is wrong. Almost anyone who senses they must reconcile their two personas, commonplace and eternal, will attempt to rediscover this part of themselves which makes possible a true and completed identity.

Journal writing is both a road towards the creative self, and an act of creativity in itself. It is a road that can show us the way home: home is where reconciliation to self takes place.

Journal writing is an accessible trip even the most housebound can take, but it is one that most people fear. Journeys characteristically either start or end with a map, often both. Travelers use a map to find their way and in the process create another map which is *their* own. In this book I hope to both provide a map for journal writing and encourage readers to make their own. All journeys carry within them seeds of the unknown. They rarely turn out exactly as we had planned them, and there is usually an unexpected detour that takes us where we were probably meant to go. I would like to break some of the barriers that keep people from this accessible journey into creative self expression.

This short book has one purpose, which is to provide a map through the obstacles people find to keeping a journal. The guide I have laid out is not complicated, or hard to follow. But only you can decide whether you want to take the trip and only you will ultimately make the map which is meant for you.

This guide to journal writing is not meant to be a textbook. It is not a primer on how to make a million dollars in Hollywood—although that could happen. It may not even clarify what is intrinsically a mysterious and marvelous process. Rather it describes, I hope, an exciting process of discovery where fear is replaced by delight and writing becomes an integral part of one's life.

There are two essential rules to keeping a journal. They are rules which apply to any undertaking. They are simple but not easy: start, and be not afraid. Starting any new project is often accompanied by fear of the unknown. This book is about banishing the fears connected with writing. It is for anyone who has felt the attraction of keeping a journal, but has not yet begun.

I offer some utilitarian suggestions on how to be comfortable in the mechanics of writing; pens, writing book, places to write, and ways in which writing can be incorporated into busy lives. There are ten exercises to be followed sequentially which will lead you into a comfortable habit of daily writing. I have quoted ideas about personal writing and excerpts from journals, memoirs and letters of famous writers to show what spaces of the human heart can be unveiled in the act of writing. I will describe how journal writing has been used critically and therapeutically to reveal and connect lives that lacked definition and integration. And finally, I have quoted from some of my own journals as a personal justification of the art of writing. For me it has become an essential way of sounding out the notes which bring into harmony my external life and interior life that, integrated, make me who I am.

Notes
from
Myself

Part I

THE JOURNAL

"At the still point of the turning world . . .
Neither from nor towards; at the still point there the
dance is . . . Except for the point, the still point, there
would be no dance, and there is only the dance."

T.S. Eliot, "Four Quartets"

It is impossible to be happy without a connected and comfortable relationship with ourselves. Nothing else works. There is only one way to establish that relationship; to go inside. A hundred transferences of ego onto someone or something else will only blur the image of self into a fading shadow of the original. Then one's God-given soul, which entered this world, "trailing clouds of glory," as Wordsworth wrote, disappears. A new love affair, a larger house, a more glamorous car; none of these clarifies the mirror of the soul without whose reflection all else is immaterial.

We are alone. This can be a frightening realization. Perhaps it is this fear, knowing we cannot rely on anything or anybody else to make ourselves whole, that is behind all excuses not to write a journal. But the sequitur to this idea that we are alone is wonderful. It means one does not have to rely on others to be happy. There are no contingent things that can destroy us once we have found our center. It is the gift awaiting anyone who will conquer their initial trepidation about journals, in whatever form it manifests itself, and just write.

The following section will cover some of the reasons why we avoid journal writing, practicalities of writing once the obstacles have been removed, and ten exercises to help you get going.

"And my shells? I can sweep them into my pocket.
They are only there to remind me that the sea recedes
and returns eternally."
—Anne Morrow Lindbergh

Chapter I

WHAT JOURNAL WRITING IS AND WHY WE AVOID IT

"As soon as I observed myself from outside myself, I recognized and understood that I had a long-standing habit of keeping an eye on myself. That's how I managed to pull myself together, over the years, checking myself from the outside."

Orhan Pamuk, *The Black Book*

These words describe the unintentional self-awareness of a character in Pamuk's book, who is concerned with the subject of identity. We too, even unknowingly, monitor ourselves in an ongoing evaluation of what is happening in our lives. Sometimes this is done so subconsciously that, like Pamuk's observer, we are hardly aware that it is happening. The benefits are negligible when we do not recognize the changes taking place. We check ourselves constantly, and what springs from this checklist is important; we can leave all information received outside, or we can internalize it, re-create it imaginatively, and only then do we get an idea of what is happening in our lives.

This is like the analogy of the piano tuner Thomas Merton uses in his book, *The Ascent to Truth*. If we do not use reason, which could be read as self-evaluation and self-knowledge, to tune the instruments of our souls, then God will not bother to play on them. "He strikes a chord and goes away. The trouble generally is that the tuner has been banging on the keys himself all day, without bothering to do the work assigned to him, which is to keep the thing in tune." It is in the examination that we begin to know ourselves, how we "stay in tune." But this work implies knowing things we would perhaps rather not know and gaining knowledge we might otherwise want to keep at bay.

"Know thyself" is as important today as it was when it was first pronounced by Greek philosophers at the acme of their civilization. Our essential human needs have not changed. We are the only species in God's creation that has been given the power of reflection and self-expression. We can consider our lives, hold them up to moral evaluation, and change them according to what we hold to be the truth. Our lives are not static, they find their courses according to the choices we make. A dog or a horse may bolt across a field, but it will not weigh the consequences of its actions, which are usually simple (food, shelter, and companionship). For us it is not so simple. We are compelled by our nature to think about our actions.

A journal lets us THINK IN WRITING and thus lets us see the full dimensions of our lives. Not just each moment as it passes, but the past and sometimes the future, seen from the present. The word is a defining aspect of our humanity. Not to use it is to throw away a gift. We are not complete if we do not use words to express who we are. Keeping a journal can bring into our lives the "breadth and the length, the height and the depth" that St. Paul described as the heightened sensibility of which we are capable. A journal is about knowing oneself. Writing one is creative, revelatory and fun!

The reasons people give for not keeping journals, even when they feel a need to do so are complex. I will try to identify and explain some of these reasons so the reader will recognize his or her own obstacles to writing.

Fear

"And that is why the man who wants to see clearly, before he will believe, never starts on the journey."

Thomas Merton, *The Ascent to Truth*

We cannot walk away from the appearance of mystery in our lives. We can never truly know when, how or from where it will come. Mystery equates with acts of grace. But it is also the unknown, and the unknown provokes fear. Fear is at the heart of escapism and may keep us from transformative encounters with mystery. A version of this almost primal fear is at work in people who want to, but cannot, get themselves to write journals.

I have seen this fear on the faces of listeners as I talked about journal writing. It expresses itself in an affectless blank look that implies, "I do not want to get involved. I do not want to get that close to myself. I am afraid of what will be revealed." A man once had the honesty to come up to me after one of my talks and say, "I am scared of what will come up if I start writing." Of course we are frightened of what we may find. But to live with unconfronted fear is worse. Not knowing who we are provokes the worst terror of all.

Credo ut intelligem—belief precedes knowledge; it is the first step. We need to make an initial leap of faith. Faith is stronger than fear, and fear is the killer of beginnings. There is probably no other word that strikes such a note of panic in the human heart as change. But change offers the possibility of discovery, and unlocking a Pandora's box of discovery opens us to growth.

The alternative to change is stasis and the slow death of the spirit.

Darwinian theory is based on the premise that change is necessary for survival. Darwin's work showed that if a living organism does not adapt, it dies. As living organisms, we are not exempt from the laws of nature. We are usually given choices; we can choose situations which are new and challenging, or we can avoid them. John Donne's well-known warning, "No man is an island unto himself," is not to be taken lightly. Journal writing allows us to discover both the island that is our self and to see the bridges connecting our island to the mainland around us. It is in this connection that we grow and adapt. Fear disconnects, and when we try to avoid it rather than facing or exploring it, we are not complete.

Time

"And my shells? I can sweep them all into my pocket. They are only there to remind me that the sea recedes and returns eternally."
Anne Morrow Lindbergh, *Gifts from the Sea*

We need reminders of eternal time to cancel out the nagging and destructive refrain, "I have no time, there are not enough hours in the day . . ." which is a common dirge in today's society. There is never enough time for work, family responsibilities and community or individual interests. Daily routines seem to become more complicated and time-consuming with new advances in technology. Communications breakthroughs have done little to simplify life or to give back time to people who are doing too much. Cellular phones, computers and E-mail are depriving us of the most crucial link of all, self to self. Today the focus is on outward connection, not inward. The result is like trying to use an extension when there is no main hook-up. It does not work. When we lack connection to ourselves we begin to disappear. Time goes so fast we vanish with it, drifting out of definition like cresting waves on a fog-blanketed beach. There is only one way to control time, and that is to slow down. One needs to stop and be with oneself for a few moments each day. Journal writing is a slowing down process, one that allows us to use time, and not become its victim.

"See, now is the acceptable time..."

2 Corinthians 6:2

Time taken moment by moment extends the hours of the day. Time extended into future problems and projects not only introduces limits, but changes our conception of the time we are in. When we only do the jobs and activities which our days call for, things always seem to fit. When we are just doing our life, we are often amazed at how much we are able to accomplish in a few hours. It is when we start worrying about shopping, when to gather children from school, or when to visit our parents that we get bogged down. We actually CAN do these things, it is dwelling on them that saps our energy.

One of the best examinations of time I have come across in my reading is in a short book entitled, *The Sacrament of the Present Moment,* by Jean-Pierre de Caussade. This is a simplifying book. It makes time management, to use a modern term, seem easy, and the benefits of time taken in "the present moment" beyond imagining. Caussade writes, "We must confine ourselves to the present moment without taking thought for the one before or the one to come." By doing this we arrive at a feeling of peace with ourselves and our lives. We also gain a feeling of surrender to the way that is meant to be, a feeling that we are part of the grand scheme, of Divine Order. "We must therefore allow each moment to be the cause of the next; the reason for what precedes being revealed in what follows, so that everything is linked firmly and solidly together in a divine chain of events."

It is only by being in the moment that one can escape that nagging harassment, "I will never get it all done." It is important to take the special moments from our planned and programmed days when they offer themselves to us. They are the gifts, and if we have trained ourselves in appreciation of the "sacred moment," whatever it brings, they can be grand and glorious gifts indeed.

To the question, "When should I keep a journal?" I reply: always. There is never a day in your life which is not worthy of description. There are times that demand more intense examination than others, times when one feels compelled to write, and other lighter moments when writing becomes an amusing conversation with oneself. At no point is our writing unworthy.

> *"It is now, in this very moment, that I can and must pay for all that I have received. The past and its load of debt are balanced against the present. And on the future I have no claim."*
>
> Dag Hammarskjöld, *Markings*

On the day of a hectic move, a friend asked me to go for a pony cart ride around the small island of Jamestown with him. Reluctantly, thinking of cartons to be opened and drawers to be lined, I accepted. When I got to my friend's farm, time suddenly switched gears. I left my car in a time without enough moments to finish all the projects I had laid out for myself. I entered into time *eternal* when I smelled the barnyard smells that have perfumed farms forever and saw the product of his labors: tiny chicks and new lambs, new plantings, endeavors which have been part of daily life for millennia.

I was given reins slippery from pony sweat, the ponies tossed their tangled, tawny manes, and we set off at a measured clip up toward the island's lighthouse. The gently beating rhythm of the drive dissolved any remaining ideas that anything had to be done on this particular day, other than to be in the day as it was.

I noticed tiny wildflowers at the side of the road because I was, in all senses, traveling slowly enough to see them. The mottled sky existed "as it was in the beginning, is now, and ever shall be," and the ocean broke on rocks it has been sculpting for millions of years. I felt childlike and happy and free.

Florida Scott-Maxwell in the journal she kept when she was an old woman, *The Measure of My Days*, describes a look on the face of her young grandchild: "Then he looks forth on the world unblinking, unhurried and with a dignity that should be the rite of Kings."

I was fortunate to have that pony cart ride on a day when I was letting time get its frantic grip on me. There are ways we can find, or ways that find us, that allow us to reclaim the "rite of Kings" which should be every man's due. "I have no time" is a poor excuse for not doing the things that show us who we are. If journal writing is one of them, then there is a way to make time for it.

> *"How can you expect to keep your powers of hearing when you never want to listen? That God should have time for you, you seem to take as much for granted as that you cannot have time for Him."*
>
> Dag Hammarskjöld, *Markings*

Privacy

"When one is a stranger to oneself, then one is estranged from others too. If one is out of touch with oneself, then one cannot touch others."
Anne Morrow Lindbergh, *Gifts from the Sea*

Privacy is not the same as isolation; the two should not be confused. Privacy can reconnect one to oneself, which in turn is a link back to the world and those you love and live with. That one seeks privacy is a sign of trying to find the strengths that affirm outward ties, not vice versa. Private moments lead us back to self, and it is from self that we gain our strengths.

As an excuse not to keep a journal, I have heard, "I do not want anyone to know my private thoughts and feelings." No one has to. A journal can remain a personal experience, or it can become a public work, evolving into an autobiography or a memoir. It is whatever one wants to make of it. The excuse of lack of privacy is usually an evasion. Whatever its basis, a denial that one can and should have a private life needs to be worked through, not avoided. Privacy is part of self-definition, which is what journal writing is all about. Private times are when we get to choose who we are going to become.

"At every moment you choose yourself. But do you choose your self? Body and soul contain a thousand possibilities out of which you can build many I's. But in only one of them is there a congruence of the elector and the elected . . . and the consciousness of the talent entrusted to you which is your I."
Dag Hammarskjöld, *Markings*

Mystery

Journal writing is associated with mystery. It is viewed as a sacred cabala open to few, a quest to be undertaken only by the chosen. Not true. Writing is, for most of us, an accessible form of self-expression. Scientists like Noam Chomsky have shown that we are born with the abilities of language firmly established in our basic mental makeup. As an extension of speech, writing is also wired into our human potential. Dag Hammarskjöld wrote in his journal, *Markings:* "Only in man has the evolution of the creation reached the point where reality encounters itself in judgment and choice." We were given language so we could judge and choose and describe ourselves. On the walls of the caves of Lascaux, in the hieroglyphs on ancient Egyptian temples, in places of belief and worship throughout the world, we have made our marks. In the words of Buddha, Confucius, the Talmud, and the Bible, we have tried to understand who we are and what we believe. It is in our nature to do so.

Children are eager to have their first diary because they are still close to themselves. They have not yet been distanced from their true selves by the complexities of life. Their writing is part of their own created world filled with dreams and fantasies. They have a direct and simple knowledge that many adults lose in the process of maturation, and they love to see themselves in their diaries. Adults have to work to regain this open self-awareness.

Studies done with young girls maturing into puberty have shown that they lose many of their natural assurances. Self-confidences that they had as children begin to disappear as the peer pressure of conformity increases with school and social commitment. Pubescent girls begin to behave less like who they are and more like who they are expected to be.

In her best-selling book, *Reviving Ophelia*, Dr. Mary Pipher describes one of her adolescent clients who "exemplifies the process of disowning the true self. With puberty she went from being a whole, authentic person to a diminished, unhappy version of herself . . . She no longer behaves in a way that meets her true needs." These are the years when the vice of conformity tightens and the corsets of fitting in begin to bind. It is often then, in the early teens or before, that girls start to keep their diaries. They need a private place where they can be themselves, and they know it. They need a retreat from their parents from whom they are beginning to separate in a natural and necessary, but not painless, way. They need their secret place, where their private and personal mysteries can be explored. For many teenage girls caught in the flux of change, their diary is the strongest connection they have to selfhood.

> *"I encourage girls to keep diaries and to write*
> *poetry and autobiographies. Girls this age love to write.*
> *Their journals are places where they can be honest and*
> *whole . . . Writing their thoughts and feelings strengthens*
> *their sense of self. Their journals are a place where their*
> *point of view on the universe matters."*

> Dr. Mary Pipher

When the fully formed public persona has emerged, molded to conventional mores and manners, the conscious need for keeping a diary disappears. It becomes less important to be one's real self than to be an acceptable member of one's community. Perhaps the confrontation between the mystery world of the diary and the blunt reality of conformity makes it uncomfortable to keep on writing. Whatever the force behind it, diary writing usually stops somewhere in the late teens for the majority of girls for whom it was a haven of retreat.

I stress girls in this discussion of youthful journal writing because I think girls tend to be more naturally introspective. But boys suffer anxiety about growing up just as girls do, and they can benefit from journal writing as well.

In all natural needs there is usually an inbuilt timing that works. Pulling away from internalized mysteries and the desire to know and explore them in journals is based on the need to integrate into the larger whole of community which will be the context of our lives. That movement away from self into others is natural and necessary, but once integrated into the larger framework, we come back to writing, to our diaries or journals, and we begin to discover our own mysteries again.

The inevitable mid-life crisis is usually accompanied by a need to explore once again—to begin that often torturous road home, back to our selves. It is often the time when we take up journal writing as a map for this transitional time in our lives. It is usually a moment when we feel the need to know our spiritual self, and if we have let this slip away in the activities of hardworking middle years, a journal is a perfect way to regain this forgotten dimension of our nature.

Dante, writing in the first book of his trilogy, *The Divine Comedy*, in his middle years finds himself lost in the dark wood of fear and doubt. He no longer knows who he is. His mentor out of darkness into light is the poet, Virgil, who leads him to the gates of paradise whole once more, completed in self-knowledge.

We each have the potential to be our own Virgil by sitting down and writing about our life. Amazing paths appear when our subconscious is released in writing. Being in the dark wood is fearful. Trying to find our way out is the sole antidote to this fear. But it is amazing the number of people who go on sitting on a cold stump in the heart of the forest, who make no effort whatsoever to move into the light. Writing is clarifying; it is not an impenetrable mystery to be avoided. Its mysteries are those of enlightenment. Exploring the mystery of our selves is a life-saving act of bravery; it is saying, "Yes, I will make discoveries, and I will take journeys offered. I will know myself."

Writer's Block

I think much resistance to writing comes from the idea that one has to be a 'writer' to write. This, combined with an apprehension that one's writing will not be good enough, that somehow it will 'fail,' can cause writer's block.

In journal writing it does not matter if one is a writer, a plumber, or an astronaut. The act of writing is obviously more enjoyable if one loves words, but it is not necessary that one be a 'writer' to keep a journal. There is no failure because anything goes and all is possible. There are no critics except yourself, and that is the critic you are trying to find.

Writer's block is often no more than another manifestation of stasis—the unwillingness to change. I know writers who will contort their personal lives like Houdini to get out of sitting down to write. They will do the most awful and boring things to avoid it. Journal writing should not be seen as a chore. It may be the only time in your day when you will be honestly judgment free. When you open your journal, you can write with abandon. That is a rare treat in this day and age. It is also therapeutic to have a place to laugh with yourself, unload secrets you've kept all day, bitch and moan if necessary, and release in ways our controlled lives often prohibit.

Before we became too delicate in our prayers, God was spoken to honestly and overtly. Injustices were ranted about, ecstasy delighted in, and all the tumult of which the human soul is capable poured forth in a bold dialogue with the Almighty. As the biblical Job's trials come to an end he converses with his

God: "Hear, I beseech Thee and I will speak: I will demand of Thee, and declare Thou unto me. I have heard of Thee by the hearing of the ear; but now mine eyes seeth Thee." (Job 42:4-5) Unlike Job we are no longer on such forthright terms of soul-baring with our Maker and have toned down our responses to conform to society's mannered constraints.

In a journal one can purge all the emotions that were bottled up during the day. Once you start, you will be amazed at just how much has been contained in the dialogue of your days. It is revelatory, therapeutic, and a great deal of fun to let loose in words, and your journal is the best, and sometimes the only, place to do it.

Much better to write out a gripe and perhaps re-evaluate its merit than to go to bed hanging onto the farthest reaches of the mattress from your spouse or lover because you have un-thinkingly let loose your grudge on him or her.

I am sure there are other blocks to journal writing, but the aforementioned are the ones I have most frequently come across in talking to people about their inability to write in spite of their interest in the idea of a journal. The following chapters will offer some simple exercises and advice which will help you work your way into a comfortable relationship with your journal. They are steps on a path. Like any other path, it will not open for you if you do not take the first step, which is to start.

Chapter II

PRACTICALITIES OF JOURNAL WRITING

"The longest part of the journey is said to be the passing of the gate."

Marcus Terentius Varro, (116-27 B.C.)

There are practical aspects to journal writing that can help in the "passing of the gate." It is important to make writing as comfortable and pleasing as possible so that it provides an open conduit to creativity. Physical comfort and aesthetic enjoyment manifest in small and seemingly inconsequential things. Minor aggravations often hold us back. The choice of book and writing instrument and place to write are important.

The Journal Book

The first practical accouterment of journal writing is the book itself. This requires some thought. If you find your journal inaccessible and uncomfortable you will not do much writing in it. The lovely hard cover book with smooth empty pages, gold ribbon marker, and angels and flowers hovering and blooming all over it may seem inspirational, but, for me, it is not very useful. The binding never gives enough for the book to lie flat, it requires two hands to keep it open, and usually only three quarters of the page is accessible for writing. In a word, for all the angels aflutter and flowers in full flush, the coffee table diary is impractical.

It may be that, for some writers, aesthetics will outweigh comfort and they will find one of these books that is worth the effort, but, for those preferring ease and accessibility, I suggest an ordinary side-spiral notebook, lined and easy to keep open. They come in wonderful colors for variety and identification. I like their neat lines, which are reminiscent of school-day discipline, but which do not impede the process of writing.

Pens and Pencils

I write with a gold Cross pen because it speeds across the lines and fits my hand perfectly. It was an extravagance I indulged in specifically for journal writing. I have written with disposable pens which have worked just as well, but this pen was a luxury I have not regretted. It is part of my pleasure in preparing to write. I like the commitment of ink. I believe in the spontaneous nature of journal writing, which does not demand correction and revision, so I prefer the more permanent markings of pen to pencil. But comfort is all, and pen or pencil it should be pleasing and chosen with care.

Time

Having a set time of the day for journal writing can be essential. It makes writing part of daily ritual, like breakfast or a shower, prayer and meditation. I write at the end of the day when I try to tie loose strings of unconnected thought and action together. Writing shows me patterns and paths that were not visible when they happened. It is a ritual of completion, and I feel something is missing in the days when I cannot sit down with my journal. When my children were younger I wrote early in the morning. Then I had time for myself before the explosions of family demands set in. One summer I routinely got up with the sun and watched it rise over a mist-milky river as I wrote trying to make sense of the feeling that I was losing myself. There have been times in my life when I have written during every spare moment I had because it was the only way I could hold chaos at bay.

It is important to find the time when writing will be the greatest treat and solace. It should not be inflexibly chiseled into your life so that it becomes another chore, like vacuuming or emptying the garbage. Journal writing is one of the delights of the day and finding the right time for it is important. Virginia Woolf wrote in her journal after tea time, and it was a treasured and honored ritual of her day.

Place

"The soul of a journey is liberty, perfect liberty to think, feel, do just as one pleases."

William Hazlitt

There are two requirements for writing: peace and privacy. It is important to find a peaceful haven—a bedroom during the daytime, a child's room during school, the kitchen after dinner has been cleaned up, even the laundry room when the machines are silent. To get space and time together in harmony may seem difficult, but, with some juggling, it can be done. I once loved writing on a deck facing a river reddened in sunrise; I now have a penchant for my kitchen at night, tea at hand. If you feel comfortable, it is the right place for you. Some of the greatest journal/memoir writing was done under constraints of freedom and privacy, in prisons and under duress and danger. Finding a place in a safe home is a luxury, not to be taken for granted.

I like to keep a small, jot-down version of my notebook in my handbag and in the car. Sometimes an unexpected wait or delay is an ideal time to write. It is a way of making use of otherwise frustrating moments. In spite of their power to facilitate ideas that seem to erupt with surprises, journals do render back to us the feeling that we are in control. And we are: we choose whether to write or not. We can wait out unexpected delays, fuming and losing gifted time, or we can keep a small book handy and enjoy the bonus free time. Seminal ideas and story plots have been written on haphazardly available bits and pieces of paper or even, as Victor Hugo reputedly did, on the scraped bark of a tree.

Attitude

*"I am seeking perhaps what Socrates asked for
in the prayer from the* Phaedrus *when he said, 'May
the outward and the inward man be at one.' . . . I would*

*like to achieve a state of inner grace from which I could
function and give as I was meant to in the eye of God."*
Anne Morrow Lindbergh, *Gifts from the Sea*

It is important to decide, as Lindbergh did, on what is essential
in one's life. At some point we must channel our energies so that
we can come as close as possible to creating the lives that rep-
resent the conscious decisions we make about who we are. We
need to know that self from which our life flows. Like icebergs
rising in frozen mist, the major part of ourselves is hidden and
submerged. We only see the fractional tip if we are not extended
in creativity.

If one approaches journal writing with abandon, amazing
things begin to happen, but to sit down and rigidly construct
what you think your day has, or should have, been leads to
inaccuracy, wishful writing and a basic hardening of self against
the mysterious side of one's nature. Without the mystery one
might as well be scrubbing the floor or emptying the garbage.

The actual events and facts of the day are important as guideposts. They are the tip of the iceberg. What marks us with our
own brand of individuality is what lies below the waterline. It
takes a certain element of surrender to the unknown to explore
beneath the surface where wholeness lies hidden.

Surrender is a crucial part of the attitude one must carry toward journal writing. It allows one to see the pieces of the puzzle
as they begin to fit into place, and the map of yet uncharted
waters take form. Florida Scott-Maxwell wrote of her own journal, "Perhaps the creating of identity is man's most essential task,
and if we demand to be given it as a right, we have not even
guessed that it is our life's work to create it."

Structure

*"Every phrase and every sentence is an end and
a beginning, every poem an epitaph . . ."*
T.S. Eliot, "Four Quartets"

Journals do not have to be structured. They do not have to pass a spelling check or a grammarians critique. But it is important to think of your writing in a critical way that will allow it to improve. The better you become at finding the right word or expressive phrase, the more you will enjoy your writing. Like all skills, and writing is most certainly a skill, practice and discipline are important. Spontaneity and abandonment are necessary, but they can also equate with sloppiness. Carelessness is a camouflage which hinders perception, and perception is what you are trying to develop.

I suggest, in the beginning especially, that one use some factual guideposts, because that is an easy and safe way to start, and it helps alleviate the panic factor inherent in any new project. Journals are a wonderful place to make an end-of-the-day inventory of changes made, feats of resolution accomplished, progress achieved, and a record of events that seem to have miraculously found their way into your 'grand scheme.' Journals are a means of identifying bad habits and noting the development of new, more productive ones. They are a good place to pat yourself on the back for a day well spent. There are many hidden indicators in the simple seeming "today I did such and such." It may not be until next week or next month that such-and-such takes on meaning. Associative processes take their own time, but they tell you a great deal about yourself. They are a true map of where you have been and where you are going, and they are the best directional signals you will probably ever get.

When you start describing your life you will find you see it more clearly. Then come the connections which occasionally allow one to see part of the pattern, the master plan. It is only revealed to us occasionally, when a few veils are pulled away for the briefest and rarest of moments. At moments like these we truly love our journals.

Florida Scott-Maxwell wrote, "What fun it is to generalize in the privacy of a notebook. It is as I imagine waltzing on ice might be. A great delicious sweep in one direction, taking you to your full strength, and then, with no trouble at all, an equally delicious sweep in the opposite direction." With all the limitations of age, writing was still fun for her! Her notebook helped her affirm and integrate her life past, present and future.

"I tried to speak to him of Alexandria, of time lost
and lost worlds . . ."
—André Aciman

Chapter III

WRITING EXERCISES

O ne of the challenges in starting any new enterprise is deciding where to start. It is one thing to decide to start, but then come the questions: Where do I begin? What do I do first? How do I do it? This chapter will offer some suggestions on how to get over this initial quandary.

Here are ten exercises that are guideline introductions to journal writing. They are meant to be suggestions, not rules, and should be adapted to suit individual needs. They are not intended to be constraining. These exercises should be used imaginatively to get you started. They are also meant to be fun.

Exercise 1

CHOOSE AN EVENT IN THE DAY

"When we are surprised at ourselves we are
being creative, and we find we can trust our own

unexpected originality . . . Creation lies in the way we get
at perception."

    D.W. Winnicott, *Home is Where We Start From*

Winnicott, an early twentieth-century psychiatrist, based his
practice on enabling "the patient to reveal himself to himself."
Journal writing is about self-revelation and perception. What we
write describes how we see ourselves and the world we live in.
The written word acknowledges the choices we are making, and
it is always a surprise if we are honest in our writing.

    The first exercise is to choose an event in your day that has
captured your imagination—something that felt as if you were
seeing it for the first time. Every day, no matter how routine,
has moments of such awareness, unless we are moving through
life in such blindness of repetition that we are not really alive
at all. Describe that particular moment of seeing in as much
detail as possible. Let go in your writing, forget sentence structure, grammar and linguistic inhibitions, and go all-out in your
description. I do not mean to suggest that grammatical rules and
the stringencies of well-used language are unimportant but you
can return to them later. In the beginning of a love affair one
can do whatever he or she wants, discipline comes later, after
the honeymoon. There are great similarities between a love affair
and journal writing: the energy of attraction guides them both.

    "God does not die on the day when we cease to
believe in a personal deity, but we die on the day when
our lives cease to be illumined by the steady radiance,
renewed daily, of a wonder, the source of which is
beyond all reason."

               Dag Hammarskjöld, *Markings*

One of my students wrote her day's entry on seeing the hot light of August burn through her daughter's bright auburn hair as she played on the beach. In all the brushings and shampooings and tying back in ribbons, she had never before seen it in a moment of pure perception when for a few brief moments of a summer's day that was all there was. She wrote about her daughter with an intertwining of love and discovery that captured those seaside moments forever. She loved the process of writing. It brought her closer to what her daughter meant to her. It is helpful in the beginning to choose a subject that attracts you in a joyful way. I would not suggest for this first exercise describing a garbage can in a dank alley, that may come later, but for now choose the golden moment.

Exercise 2

WHAT WERE THE SURPRISES IN YESTERDAY'S ENTRY?

The second exercise is to re-read yesterday's entry and write about surprises you found in your writing. Did it reveal anything about yourself that you were not aware of? Did any hidden interests or uncharted paths show up that you feel like pursuing? How do you see yourself in what you chose to write about? What does your writing say about who you are? You may find the answers to these questions are not what you expected.

These are the surprises of creation that Winnicott referred to. My student who wrote about her daughter's hair was surprised that she had chosen the subject of her daughter. She was going through a difficult stage in her life and thought she was disappearing in the act of motherhood. When she re-read her entry she understood that being a mother was what she had chosen to do, and that she was not disappearing. On the contrary, she was doing exactly what she was supposed to be doing at this time in her life.

Writing allows us to distance ourselves from the actions and thoughts of our day so that we can view them with reflection. Looking at, as well as being in, our life we see it in all its dimensions. Once you have re-read the first entry from yesterday, describe your reaction to it and what surprised you. What would you like to pursue in the light of your discoveries? Virginia Woolf, describing why she kept a journal, wrote, "because one never realizes an emotion at the time." Her daily writing allowed her to access her emotions and see them in full awareness with the completed dimensionality of description.

E x e r c i s e   3

EXTEND AN EVENT INTO THE CONTEXT OF A WHOLE DAY

Extend your descriptions so they reflect your whole day, not just one episode or thought from it. Look at your writing and the words you are choosing, and start to get rid of any loose ends which I may have seemed to encourage in the beginning. Though it may have been necessary for initial fluidity of writing it will not help you to gain journal writing proficiency. A wonderful feeling of gratification suffuses one, like an unexpected compliment, on finding just the right descriptive word or phrase.

When you have finished your entry re-read it and note the hidden surprises you find that are indicators of what has attracted you. The skeleton of your true self is emerging. It is still 'an emperor in his new clothes' perhaps, but the clothing will come. The naked self will be vested in the finest of raiments, and you will have stitched them.

You have begun. By now there may be a sense of completeness surfacing in your writing. Describing the whole day enables
you to see how individual events melt into the process of your
entire life. The special event you chose for the first exercise came
to your mind for a reason, because of its significance in the grand
scheme which, little by little, does begin to show itself, if we
pursue it.

Exercise 4

FIND AN INTRODUCTORY FORMULA
FOR YOUR DAILY WRITING

Since starting is often the hardest part of any new endeavor,
working out an introductory formula to get your day's entry
focused is important. The impressionist painter Eugène Boudin
marked his canvases with the climatic conditions of the day on
which he began his new work, including the wind direction and
velocity. He was one of the first of the impressionist painters
who sought direct contact with changing light in nature, and
weather was important to his vision and art.

Whatever acts as a focal point of your day is a good way to
begin your journal entry. It could be line and color which pulls
your eye first thing in the morning and gives rhythm to your
perception, it may be sounds and silences that orchestrate your
actions. Whatever attracts you is what will work in finding an
introduction to your daily writing. Try several approaches and
see which one feels most comfortable and draws you to it. I
always start with the most prosaic and mundane subject—the
weather. Weather affects my mood and perception and, for me,
is a natural lead into description of what has happened in my
day, unusual, lovely or awful—and from there I am off and writ-

ing. Many people remember dreams which deeply affect the beginning of their day. Sometimes memories of the previous day linger, unfinished, needing a written resolution. Some of us have morning meditations and readings that stay in our mind as guidelines for the rest of the day. Whatever it may be, it is very helpful to have an automatic, kick-in to your day's writing.

Exercise 5

LANGUAGE—DISCOVER YOUR OWN LEXICON

Now is the time to think of language, to develop your own lexicon and choose the syntax you work with. It is important to keep spontaneity in your writing, but it is also important to discover how rewarding it is to find the right word for what you want to say. The more you write, the easier it will become to create the definition you are looking for.

Writing is not an overnight miracle. Like all creative acts, it takes work and time. What does happen almost immediately is you will find yourself writing of things you did not know were on your mind. Journal writing arouses the subconscious and brings forth unexpected revelations which show us who we are without camouflage. We wear a great deal of defensive gear as we go through our days. It is no wonder our lives often appear to be battlegrounds where we wander dazed in fatigue. Journal writing is returning to a protected camp, stripping off one's armor and being our real and unembattled selves. It is easy to get so used to the armor that you do not even notice its weight and ugliness anymore—until you strip it off.

In this exercise look for one idea or phrase that has surprised you, and has probed into a place that had been hidden from you. Thinking about the words you are using and the flow of your written language, enlarge on the idea. Using both free, natural writing and the discipline of created language, try to find your linguistic voice. It is a true expression of yourself.

Language tells us a great deal about ourselves. Often we do not use it as imaginatively as we might in our daily speech or in the formalities and abbreviations of business and household activities. We pare language down to its skeleton and, fleshless, it often denies us its full grandeur. We rarely get to see and hear language decked out and tarted up for special occasions. In journals we can listen with our inner ear and hear the unusual words, expressions and descriptions which are our own way of reflecting on life as we perceive it. In our notes to ourselves we can use those *Readers Digest* query words we know, but seldom utter, and be as grandiose, or bawdy, or poetic as we want to be.

Allegory fell by the wayside soon after the Middle Ages, but we can regain medieval vision by looking for allegory and symbolism in our daily lives. When we use these images in our journals, we begin to find our own language patterns. Yesterday as I walked on a perfect December day I 'saw' a whole battlefield scene play out in the lightly clouded sky where it seemed the clouds arcing across the heavens were rows of longbows, an army of archers aiming their missiles at an infinite and endless horizon. The ocean pranced onto the beach steaming, foaming with spume, pounding in its charge of white crested waves—a Saracen army? The target of the heavenly longbows? Imagination run riot perhaps, but metaphors do create splendid images. I take the same walk almost every day—I never see the same images.

Many people have a naturally poetic imagination which they have to stifle in the course of ordinary days. A journal is a wonderful place to let one's real voice sound out, in poetry, in song and verse, in the full reaches of one's creative energies.

The Japanese have used a form of journal writing since the eighth century which expresses itself in poetry. It is highly personal and emotive writing. These journalists view time as process, flow, and part of the natural cycle. It is a different orientation from the west. For us time is composed of events, but for these Japanese poets events happen in time. These art diaries do not hinge on fact, they incorporate the fictional into the entire reality of their writing. The author of *The Tosa Diary* wrote, "Art is that which is created when we are unable to suppress our feelings." The formality of daily entry was loosened into a more flexible system geared to incorporate and express emotion. Feelings are not necessarily bound by a twenty-four hour time span; these Japanese journals are not regimental daily writing, rather, they are ongoing creative expressions and unique in journal literature. Not all of us may be up to the articulate writing of Izumi Shikibu in his diary, but it is nice to know that if so inspired a journal is a place we CAN begin to reveal our poetic soul.

> *"Though I have seen*
> *Such wonders as the surging waves*
> *High upon Mount Matsu,*
> *The long rain that I beheld today*
> *Surpasses the waves beyond belief."*
> Izumi Shikibu

Exercise 6

FIND PATTERNS IN YOUR WRITING

> *"It is not the desert island nor the stony*
> *wilderness that cuts you from people you love. It is the*
> *wilderness in the mind, the desert wastes in the heart*
> *through which one wanders lost and a stranger."*
> Anne Morrow Lindbergh, *Gifts from the Sea*

The theme of Lindbergh's book was retrieval of self on a lonely beach, searching for shells, the outside of her life, in the hope they would give her vital clues to the inside self she was hoping to reclaim.

In the entries of the last five days, see if you can find a current in your writing which indicates a distinct flow of thought. How do you see yourself in your journal? What mirrors are becoming newly reflective? What is attracting you to describe them? Nothing holds more energy than attraction; it is the magnet to your real self. It will give direction and show where you are meant to go. Select an event or observation you have written about and describe how the unmirrored action or thought changed in your writing, how action translated into words is helping you see your life in broader dimensions.

André Aciman, in his book *Out of Egypt*, describes his last night in Alexandria, a city he had grown up in and loved.

> *"And suddenly I knew, as I touched the damp,*
> *grainy surface of the seawall, that I would always*
> *remember this night, that in years to come I would*
> *remember sitting there, swept with confused longing as I*
> *listened to the water lapping the giant boulders beneath*
> *the promenade and watched the children head toward the*
> *shore in a winding, lambent procession. I wanted to come*
> *back tomorrow night, and the night after, and the one*
> *after that as well, sensing that what made leaving so*
> *fiercely painful was the knowledge that there would never*
> *be another night like this, that I would never eat soggy*
> *cakes along the coast road in the evening, not this year*
> *or any other year, nor feel the baffling, sudden beauty of*
> *that moment when, if only of an instant, I had caught*
> *myself longing for a city I never knew I loved."*

Have you, like Aciman, discovered something that you love that you never knew you loved? In what new places is love revealing itself? Where does attraction lead?

Exercise 7

How Did These Patterns Manifest Themselves?

This is an extension of the previous exercise. Look at the mirrored image of yourself revealed in your journal. How did this image appear? Did it happen by a process of slowing down, and was it necessary to prioritize in order to make time for your writing? Writing is like getting off a "bullet train" onto an old-fashioned, slow-moving train that stops at all local stations. You can see where you are going, you have stopping points for observation, and there are many arrivals along the way, not one faraway destination that may seem unreal in its distance. By identifying the ways in which these new mirrored images of yourself have appeared you may find small or large changes in your life you would like to make permanent. Describe these changes using the defining words and phrases which you think make your writing your own. This is a form of daily inventory in which you can observe progress in changes you wish to make in yourself and in your life.

Journal writing is a way of putting cognitive therapy to work on your own. If you see there are obvious misalignments in your thoughts, you can make the necessary adjustments to bring your life into a more coherent pattern. Once aware of a problem, as you are when it confronts you in your own written words, then it becomes easier to think into being the changes you would like to see effected in your life. It is difficult, if not impossible, to change when what you want changed remains undefined. Journal writing is one of the blocks upon which therapeutic work and counseling rest. It is one of the most effective ways in which we reveal the truth about ourselves. Whether we are working on minor shiftings of our lives or are engaged in a major overhaul, what we write to ourselves on a daily basis can be at the heart of healing. In *Reviving Ophelia*, Dr. Pipher distinguishes between young girls "who stay connected to their true selves" and those who get lost and separated from who they truly are. The girls who stay connected "think about their experiences. They do not give up on trying to resolve contradictions and make connections between events. They may seek out a parent, teacher or therapist to help them. They may read or write in a journal. They will make many mistakes and misinterpret much of reality, but girls with true selves make a commitment to process and understanding their experiences." Of one patient she writes, "Lori was particularly good at looking within herself to make decisions. She thought through issues and decided what was best for her. After that she was relatively immune to peer pressure. She was steering, not drifting, determined to behave in ways that made sense to her."

Therapy is work, and journal writing can sometimes seem too much work when we find ourselves writing about problems in our lives. But it is work well worth the doing. Sometimes we need to make a complete 180° shift in our lives, sometimes only a degree or two is required. Whichever it may be, journals are a means by which it can happen. We owe it to ourselves to make this great source of clarification available. Using them we can steer our lives so they do not drift away.

Exercise 8

WHAT TO DO WHEN YOU DO NOT WANT TO WRITE

This exercise is for the times when you do NOT want to write. And they will happen. There are days when inspiration is the last thing going on in one's head. This is when the entry format becomes helpful. Just sit down and write, about the weather, or the basic events of your day. It is important to keep your journal going. Do not let your writing stop. Write anything, not as if an executioner's sword were hanging over your head, but just to keep the engine turning over. If you stop, it will be hard to break the halt and start again. It is sometimes in these moments of creative depletion that you can recharge yourself in ways you did not know you possessed. Then you will know why journal writing is important, and how it is creative. You may not come to this exercise for days or months, but when you do, describe writing when you did not want to write. How did you start? And what did you discover?

Resistance can be as revealing as volition. It indicates obstacles and lets us see our own particular sinkholes before we fall into them. Blocks of any kind leave one in a state of lethargy and weave webs of inertia around even the most active lives. When we are faced with a project we don't feel like tackling and we back away from it, the result is we usually get hit by paralysis which invades other areas of our lives. If I leave clothes at the cleaners after they are ready, or lay aside bills and letters, I find extensions of this procrastination invading other areas of my life that have nothing to do with clean sweaters or the telephone company. Everything begins to seem off, and I feel as if I am not accomplishing anything. The same holds true of established routines which we have decided to undertake because we know they will be beneficial, if we stop them for no good reason we are going to feel guilt. Acute appendicitis is a valid excuse not to write in one's journal; a lazy mood or an uninspired day is NO EXCUSE AT ALL. Often it is exactly when one is suffering from a bout of ennui that forcing oneself into activity is the way back into a re-energized state. There are great rewards to be gained from this seemingly forced labor, not least of which is just keeping going. The real plus is finding out why you didn't want to write, which you will in your own words, and the discovery of what perhaps you thought you did not want to discover. Writing through blocks is a creative process; waiting for them to pass never works. Conquering the blockages, which we all have, is immeasurably satisfying. It is an empowering way to deal with lassitude in all its many devious forms.

Exercise 9

EXPLORE AN AREA OF UNCOMFORTABILITY

Now that you are hopefully at ease with the process of journal writing, try to describe an area of discomfort in your life. Explore something that is not as you would like it to be, and see what is revealed in your description. You will find clarifications and even solutions that will surprise you. If you are absolutely honest in your writing, you will have a better idea of where you are and where you are going after describing this area of dissatisfaction. Obtaining critical distance makes problems more manageable. It is when we allow the vultures of unexamined life to screech their way through our thoughts that we get into trouble. It is possible, through writing, to tame these vultures so they become interesting, if not beautiful. There are "dark nights of the soul" that are as much a part of us as sunlit mornings. If not treated as part of growth, they will destroy us. Like language, these dark nights are given to us for a reason. Through language they can be understood.

The "prison" journals I shall discuss in a later chapter are excellent examples of writing done under duress. Bad times as well as good need definition and incorporation into the whole of our selves. Often one of the rewards of these "dark nights" and the "winters of discontent" is that they do rouse us to reaction and response in order to survive, and we often find parts of ourselves which remain untouched in happier, easier times. The triumph of survival and knowledge of one's fortitude cannot be known until tested. We need to write about our desert wasteland experiences or they vanish and we have suffered for no gain.

Exercise 10

WHAT HAVE YOU DISCOVERED?

"My job is definitely to be myself."
D.W. Winnicott, "Home is Where We Start From"

"Life is its own journey, presupposes its own change and movement, and one tries to arrest them at one's eternal peril."

Laurens Van der Post

As a final exercise describe what you have discovered thus far in journal writing. What have been the surprises? Where does your creativity lie? What has writing done to your perception of yourself? Compare your first and last entry and see how you have developed a style and language of your own.

The dictionary definition of "create" is "to cause to exist, bring into being." In the course of these ten exercises, in finding your own vocabulary and means of expression, you have entered into an act of creation. And what has been created, by acknowledging problems and seeking solutions, is your *self*. Winnicott, who I quoted at the beginning of this chapter, claimed that the goal of therapy is "to enable the patient to reveal himself to himself." Thus "Creativity is then the doing that arises out of being. It indicates that he who is, is alive." If we are not creative, we are left abandoned with "the feeling that nothing means anything, of futility, I couldn't care less."

We need the awareness of self which lies in creativity in order to access all the other dimensions of life. Discovering internal mysteries allows us to see the external ones. The core of self is that often ghostlike quality which is utterly personal. Only in the creative act do the ghosts of self take on identifiable forms. We all have the ability to materialize these ghosts of self, and in these ten exercises you must have seen some of them take shapes you had never before seen. To quote Winnicott once more, "Somewhere in the scheme of things there can be room for everyone to live creatively. This includes retaining something personal, perhaps secret, that is unmistakably yourself." The secrets are often the best part, but it is work getting to them.

It is helpful to make a list of the reasons why keeping a journal has been useful to you. This list serves as a reminder when one is tempted to abandon what may seem just one more routine in an overloaded day. This list also serves as an outline of one's journal keeping habits and a description of the form and style that is best suited to one's individual writing needs.

Journals are above all flexible. It is exactly this mutability which is one of their greatest assets, as it allows and demands of us that we become fluid and capable of change. For the control freak (which I would label about 95% of my acquaintances, friends and relatives and in which category I include myself)

journals are an invaluable voice of reality, singing out the wonderful nature of change. Nothing is ever exactly the same twice
around, and, for the controlling person who wants duplicate results time after time, a journal is a necessary reminder that it
doesn't work that way. If we let events happen and take the time
to write about chance as well as planned occurrences in our lives,
we can see a much larger pattern evolving, one which extends
way beyond the scope of a twenty-four hour day. We can see
what at first glance may appear to be random events and responses in our lives as a manifestation of chaos, or we can take
these seemingly random moments in our lives as part of a coherent if not always comfortable whole.

Journal writing is one of the best ways I know to take oneself
out of chaos into pattern. Like a magical pad children use where
words seem to surface out of a blank page, order does appear
through our writing. I never know what I will write until I have
written it, and I have found in my journal at least the truth,
which allows me to know why I act the way I do. Times of crisis
or turmoil are unavoidable, they are unbearable unless one can
work them into the larger framework of one's life. Journals allow
that enlarging to take place. They shrink the epic proportions
of crisis as well as clarify them.

One summer I used Miracle-Gro full strength on my roses and
nearly killed them. The more-is-better approach can be deadly;
if I had read the instructions and diluted the chemical it would
have been just fine. There are times in our life that need dilution,
a way to spread the intensity so it does not kill us.

Journals let that diffusing happen. The killer dramas blend out
into a larger pattern beyond their momentary lives and become
incorporated into the picture of ourselves.

The "grand scheme" is a vision that only comes if we work to
see it. Journal writing is part of the work we can do to put
change on the plus side of the register and learn to recognize it
for the necessary and delightful part it plays in our development.

For those of us who sometimes find the surprise element in our lives hard to deal with, journal writing helps us learn to recognize our creativity and enjoy our surprises, which could be called blessings.

Self-examination is an art, it manifests itself wherever the soul finds its correspondences. If you have made it this far you are probably seeing your creative, real self appearing. You can congratulate yourself for having dared to make the quest. And you can take comfort in the knowledge that, piece by piece, the puzzle will come together.

"All the names which the soul gives to God, it receives from the knowledge of itself."

Meister Eckhart, "Meditations"

Part II

Journal Writing Past to Present: Opening the Door

"Do not regret the passing of the camel and the caravan."
—William Langewiesche

"What man can teach another to understand this truth? What angel can teach it to an angel? What angel can teach it to a man? We must ask it of you, seek it in you; we must knock at your door. Only then shall we receive what we ask and find what we seek; only then will the door be opened to us."

Saint Augustine, *Confessions*

Writing in question-and-answer form is a way of knocking on the door to self-knowledge. Augustine knew where the answers lay and he wrote his *Confessions* as both question and response. Have we, close to two centuries later, forgotten this essential means of communication?

Self, the independently introspective self of our era is a new phenomena and the diary/journal as a private vehicle of self-expression is a modern development. Until the sixteenth century people saw themselves in conjunction with their environment, connected to their community, their family, their status in a hierarchically arranged society, and to their God. The versions of 'personal writing' which predated what we now think of as journal writing, were outwardly oriented. They were documentary as well as self-exploratory; they were meant to be shared. Man had not split from the cosmos or from the society into which he had been born.

The etymology of the word 'journal' derives from the late Latin word *diurnalis* (daily). In Old French and Middle English it carried through as the breviary, a book of hymns, offices and prayers for the canonical hours of the day. Writing, study and the notations of daily life were in the hands of the clergy who had access to books and the passing on of written tradition. That the scholastic movement of the late Middle Ages took place under the auspices of the church is no coincidence—churches and monasteries were centers of learning until the Renaissance.

The predecessors of today's journal were commonplace books listing daily events and household activities, account books of credit and debit, and books of hours which scheduled the year according to ecclesiastical pattern. One of the most beautiful of these is the sublimely illustrated *Très Riches Heures du Duc de Bary*.

Travel diaries were not merely sentimental souvenirs, but records of exploration. Ships' logs, maps, and charts of newly discovered territories recorded the Age of Exploration. Richard Hakluyt's *Voyages* was a description of the discoveries made by 16th-century pioneers and had nothing to do with the internal journeys which the word now conjures up to the psychologically oriented, late 20th-century mind. There was little sentiment in these documents.

In the mid-17th century the first diary was published by Samuel Pepys. From 1660 to 1669 Pepys wrote a raft of entries on a daily basis covering the events of his career in the admiralty, the quotidian ups and downs of his domestic life both in and outside of marriage, and a description of the three great catastrophes of the decade: the great plague, the fire of London, and the Dutch fleet sailing up the Thames. He explored his emotions and reactions to these events making his journal a private vehicle as well as a public document.

Within a hundred years the journal had come into its own, and James Boswell cemented its permanence with his 1785 publication of *Journal of a Tour to the Hebrides* describing his Scottish tour of 1778 with Dr. Samuel Johnson. Boswell's great biography *The Life of Samuel Johnson, L.L.D.* was soon to follow. From then on journal and diary, memoir and autobiography, have become one of the most useful and malleable forms of writing we indulge in. The format of journal/diary in our post-Pepys era has been used to document, analyze, fantasize, and generally serve the diverse needs of the human heart. The uses (and abuses) of the genre are extensive.

Two journals, in particular, are among my favorites and in my mind are excellent examples of a journal/diary as revelation of the writer's self within the context of his time. They are early, pre-Pepys, and they are as revealing of the human heart as any writing I know of. One is the *Meditations* of Marcus Aurelius, the other is the *Confessions* of Saint Augustine.

The *Meditations* were originally called *To Himself*. They were written circa A.D. 167 when Marcus Aurelius, then emperor of Rome, was in the Danube region with his legions trying to control the barbarian invasion of the empire. He wrote these meditations as a commonplace book of ideas. They turned out to be his credo, the heart of all he believed in, and an unveiling of his innermost self. There is a very different rendering of ego in his writing than we would expect to find now in the post-Freudian, egocentric world we live in. What makes this small book meaningful is the writer's invention of himself through his journal writing. For Marcus Aurelius inside was inextricably connected to his outside. Unlike Descartes, he would never write "cogit ero sum." (I think, therefore I am.) He *thought* in order *to act*, as well as *to be*. His life was expressed in action; "A little flesh, a little breath, and a Reason to rule all—that is myself." (Book II)

Marcus was a Stoic in a day when philosophy was religion, and Stoicism was the religion of the upper classes. He begins his notations, *To Himself*, with a quotation from the guiding light of Stoicism Cleanthes; "To us alone of all that lives and moves upon the earth is granted a voice and an utterance." He listened to that voice and used his internally perceived knowledge to direct his outward life. He travels inward in order to make the necessary outward connections and writes both: "Remember, it is the secret force hidden deep within us that manipulates our strings; . . . there, we might even say, is the man himself," and "As a part you inhere in the Whole." In what was probably an extreme of human isolation as emperor in the far hinterlands of his empire, Marcus Aurelius stayed connected—to himself and the larger whole which he thought of as the "Divine Unity."

His reminders to himself could come from the most contemporary cognitive therapy handbook: "Your mind will be like its habitual thoughts; for the soul becomes dyed with the color of its thoughts." He demonstrates a practical as well as humorous approach to 'public relations' which must have been a large part of his difficult job when he writes: "Men exist for each other. Then either improve them, or put up with them." He wrote "The properties of a rational soul are these. She can contemplate herself, analyze herself, make of herself what she will . . ." This is exactly what Marcus Aurelius did in his *Meditations* which are as accessible and valid to the reader now as they were almost two centuries ago.

Saint Augustine's *Confessions*, written in the 4th century A.D., has an immediacy which makes the writer come alive. The book is a triple confession: of the writer's past sin and error, of new found faith, and of God's glory. With the sacramental overtones of the word 'confession' a modern-day reader could suppose themselves in for a highly theological and personally removed discussion of religious faith. Nothing could be more contrary to what one will find in the pages of Augustine's *Confessions*. What makes it a highly accessible book is its frankness and its childlike honesty in what is a fluid, open and forthright conversation between Augustine and his God. The reader sees the working of his heart;

> *"These books served to remind me to return to my own self. Under Your guidance I entered into the depths of my soul, and this I was able to do because Your aid befriended me. I entered, and with the eye of my soul, such as it was, I saw the Light that never changes casting its rays over the same eye of my soul, over my mind."*

Memory is one of his major themes, it is the cloister into which he escapes for signs of himself. He writes for the same reasons we write, to explore ourselves in memory. "The mind and the memory are one and the same. In it I meet myself as well."

Augustine's definition of time, which is a seamless convergence of past, present and future is echoed remarkably closely in T.S. Eliot's first lines of "Burnt Norton." (Part one of the poem, "Four Quartets.")

> *"Time present and time past*
> *Are both perhaps present in time future*
> *And time future contained in time past."*

Augustine's description of time explains why we must keep account of the present and may be one of the most lucid, contemporary and healthy definitions of time ever written:

> *"If the future and the past do exist, I want to*
> *know where they are. I may not yet be capable of such*
> *knowledge, but at least I know that wherever they are,*
> *they are not there as future or past, but as present. For*
> *if, wherever they are, they are future, they do not yet*
> *exist; if past, they no longer exist. So wherever they are*
> *and whatever they are, it is only by being present that*
> *they are."*

The entire lovely book of *Confessions* is not only a three layered confession, but a series of questions asked of the Almighty as friend and teacher and knower of all. It is only in questioning and receiving answers that we can live, grow and become. Parsifal was the only knight to be granted knowledge of the Grail— he alone questioned the Fisher King. In writing we not only question, we also receive the occasional answer. The *Confessions* have as much bearing on our own queries as they did almost two centuries ago and can still open doors for us.

J o u r n a l s   b y   A r t i s t s

The tradition of journal writing has seen many varied exemplaries in the centuries since Marcus Aurelius and Saint Augustine. It is a genre not confined to writers alone as artistic currents often converge, and many dancers, painters and musicians have found the journal/memoir a compelling outlet for their artistic aspirations.

Among the long list of painter-as-journalist, the following are those I have enjoyed the most:

The notebooks of Leonardo da Vinci have a commonbook appearance and are filled with fantasy and imagination run riot, with sketches and drawings showing his art in that fluid and intense moment when it is still between artistic vision and crafted reality.

The written journals of Eugène Delacroix contain his unequivocal points of view and present a black-and-white universe of absolutes:

> *"The modern style is bad."*
> *"Find that I dislike Paris as much as ever."*
> *"Custom dulls the edge of our sensations."*
> *"Grey is the enemy of all painting."*

His sketchbook journal of a trip taken with the Conte de Mornay to Morocco, on the other hand, is the polar opposite—a spontaneous combustion showing light-filled and color-blazed form which foreshadowed the Impressionists. These jotted observations of color, light, and Arabic life are flying sketches, sense impressions, which Delacroix used in later paintings. He writes:

"The main source of interest comes from the soul
of the artist; that is the paramount quality for an artist,
and no less essential for an art lover."

A few decades later impressionism inspired painters who expressed themselves in word as well as art. Edgar Degas, Paul
Gauguin and Vincent van Gogh all kept notebooks and journals
revealing their thoughts and visions which gave rise to highly
personalized styles, both discovering and showing themselves in
their writing as well as their paintings.

The *Notebooks of Edgar Degas* contain drafts of landscapes and
horses and ballet dancers with jottings in the margins. They were
his workbook and the edges are filled with addresses and time-
tables, quotations from *The Bible* and books he was reading as
well as his reflections on such subjects as light and color and
future work projects.

Paul Gauguin's *Noa Noa* describes his journey from France to
Tahiti and what he hoped to achieve in this radical readjustment
of environment. He went to Tahiti so "that I would know"—
know himself and get to know the wellsprings from which his
art arose in a primitive society where he hoped he could get the
native people to trust him. Paris in its late 19th century flurry
of modernization was enervating him, as it was Delacroix and
many of the painters of this period who found they needed a
more peaceful and quiet environment to work in.

The letters of Vincent van Gogh to his brother Theo, and
Theo's return letters to Vincent, resemble a journal in dialogue
form, expressing a heartrending need for communication and
understanding. There are few more honest descriptions of a tor-
tured artistic soul than these letters of an artist trying to find his
way, exploring the nuances of his creative expression and attempting desperately to keep his sanity. Sanity was elusive and
the struggle to hang on was expressed in Vincent's letters to his

brother, along with his thoughts on his art and his preoccupation with the art market and the salability of his paintings.

Journals by Dancers

Dancers are often volatile of temperament and personality, and many have kept journals to give yet another dimension to their artistic expression. One of the most intense, erotic and emotionally revealing of these dancer's journal/diaries is that of Vaslav Nijinsky, anguishing over his relationship with his lover, mentor, and artistic director Sergei Diaghilev.

Martha Graham's journal writings were intended as an aid in the writing of her autobiography, but became so interesting in and of themselves that they were published as her *Notebooks*. These books move in a fast and abbreviated form, a written dance, which is a melange of meditations, observation and imagination before it took form in dance. They allowed her to express many of the ideas which later were to be developed in her choreography.

George Balanchine and his protégé, Suzanne Farrell, have left us their personal accounts of the Balanchine era of the American Ballet Theatre. Rudolf Nureyev perhaps created more mystery in his accounting of his life than he unveiled, but that was his nature. Fantasy and imagination, the melting together of real and surreal had great appeal for him and the reader of his diaries is never quite sure when one begins and the other takes over. Dissimulation is part of the dancer's art.

Journals by Scientists

Scientists are also creators, and many have left journal records that are an amalgam of self and discovery, emotion and hard fact.

Albert Einstein has written some of the most revealing lines in any journal of any time. *Wonder and Awe*, his necessary and meaningful components of a life worth living, have become bywords in describing the essentials of human response to life.

Charles Darwin's *Beagle* diaries, written when he was voyaging through the Galapagos Islands and South America young and as yet undefined, were the working ground for his *Origin of the Species*. Although much of his journal notation is of a scientific nature, there are hints of the fragility of body and mind that were to constrain him throughout his life, landing him in sanitariums and retreats to recuperate from both real and neurasthenic maladies. He was treading on God's turf when he started questioning (and answering) the mystery of man's origins, and his consequent anxiety over moral rightness and social and academic acceptance often left him debilitated. Darwin lets his readers know the price to be paid for opening new intellectual vistas.

Travel Journals

Travel journals in the post-Pepys era usually have a highly defined and individualistic perspective from which the traveler observes new territories.

In his *Democracy in America* of 1835, Alexis de Tocqueville used his own political viewpoint to analyze and understand the American system which he observed while on a tour to report on the penal system of the United States. Prior to this he had kept an extensive diary of his *Journey to England and Ireland*. He was a politician, and political values were primarily what he so brilliantly observed and reflected on in his travels.

A later day French traveler to the United States, Simone de Beauvoir, saw what she wanted to see ideologically and failed to change any of the preconceived ideas she had formed of the new country she visited. In 1947 she wrote *America Day by Day* and passed the America she saw on her travels through the sieve of her own moral consciousness producing a moralistic critique which had everything to do with Simone de Beauvoir and very little to do with the realities of her experience of America. She seems to be seeking confirmation, not exploration or revelation of the new in her travels. She would probably have done better to have stayed at home.

André Maurois took the opposite tack in his book *From My Journal* and proclaimed the benefits of open-mindedness in observing a new country. He makes a conscious and concerted effort not only to see the new and try to understand it, but to see the good in it. He is a true tourist; he seeks to be "instructed," which the American Heritage Dictionary defines as "to tour."

Journals by Novelists

Many writers have used their journals as workbooks for their published writing, as well as emotional sounding boards and outlets for their inner lives.

Albert Camus' *Cahiers* holds some of the first images of his published works, and thoughts and phrases like "Aujourd'hui maman est morte," ("Today mother died.") the memorable opening line of *The Stranger*, appear in his cahier notebook. This fluid movement from journal to finished work gives a feeling of immediacy to his writing, making his fiction seem as if it was the actuality of his life—as in fact was often the case.

Graham Greene's 1959 *The Congo Journal*, holds the skeleton of what would become the novel, *A Burnt Out Case*. His journal is filled with a myriad of small observations and details, and he admitted to being "like a careful housewife, who is unwilling to throw away anything that might serve its turn."

Victor Hugo, who always kept a notebook in his pocket and was reputed to have written on a tree bark in a moment of paperless inspiration, was known for turning away in the middle of a conversation to make notes which invariably found their way into the vast number of novels and stories that make up his published work.

Feodor Dostoyevsky kept three notebooks concurrently with the writing of *Crime and Punishment* which he saw itself as a form of diary. In the notebooks he outlined the larger framework of his novel as well as noting the minutiae of psychological detail which make it the fascinating and successful novel it is.

Franz Kafka's journals contain the alpha and omega of his ideas for his work and strangely in-depth psychological interpretations of himself and his admittedly claustrophobic universe. He questioned himself in his journal and he sought answers from it—answers to the complexities of himself and answers to how he would work out the published writing which was to evolve from that self.

A journal/diary is a perfect place to experiment and try out ideas in the freedom of the moment without deadlines and publishers imposing on one's creative imagination. I cannot imagine a writer's life without this form of daily and informal notation. Getting the finished work together demands disciplines other than the unrestricted writing of a journal.

The freedom of journal writing and the rigid scheduling of

obligations complement each other and work well together, so
it is no surprise that writer and journal often go hand-in-glove.

Period Journals

Frequently, journal writers become so identified with the period
in which they write that they come to be seen as the written
embodiment of their times:

Jonathan Edwards' account of his life and spiritual trials in the
colonial America of the 1720s *was* the pilgrim experience.

The Goncourt brothers, Edmond and Jules, *are* the literary
world of 19th century France, in their comments, gossip and
repartee of the social and political life of their period. Their
notes and commentary reflect the very essence of their time.

Henri Beyle Stendhal's six "romantic" journals are the heart
and soul of the romantic period which captured England and the
European continent in its dream world at the end of the 19th
century. His tendency to narrow the world into his own private
universe of angst and emotion is one we still cling to.

Meriwether Lewis' and William Clark's extensive journal records the exploration of western North America, and *is* the pio-
neer experience.

Queen Victoria's *Highland Journals* of 1868 and 1883 are the
quintessence of the Victorian dichotomy between passion and
repression. They read very much like the journals of any tourist
thrilled and impressed with nature and daily events. The occasional politically minded entry is an exception from her real self
on holiday.

In his World War I diary, Siegfried Sassoon expressed the
desperate alienation of the young men of his generation faced
with near extinction in senseless trench warfare. His journal af-
forded him a tenuous hold on a world which was fast disap-

pearing, and an identity he at times no longer recognized as his own. In his journal he wrote, "There was something between these pages which anyhow couldn't be taken away from me." It provided him with a grip on his identity when sanity had seemed to disappear.

The period between the great wars has perhaps never been as well described as in the journals of Sir Harold Nicolson, published by his son Nigel. They give the reader a portrait of a strange union, (his marriage to Vita Sackville-West), an insider's description of the politically volatile events of the time, and a gossipy account of a fertile period of eccentricity.

Evelyn Waugh's volumes of journals and letters border on the edge of that eccentricity in what is a "Who's Who" of the age. He was funny, outrageous and brutally harsh in his commentary, which unfortunately had a tendency, as he aged, to become jaundiced and unnecessarily cruel as he drank himself into alienated misery. His penchant for self-obliteration is nowhere more evident than in a letter to his son whom he enviously admonished to "enjoy the anesthesia, dear boy" during some minor surgery he had to undergo.

Virginia Woolf belongs to this prolific journal writing period and wrote thirty volumes of diaries in the years 1915 to 1941. Her writing had less political content than that of Nicolson or Waugh; it was more of a personal accounting of the extreme conflicts of her uneasy nature. Her diaries make wonderful reading for anyone interested in the process of journal writing as she discusses the pros and cons of her daily writing as they pertain to both her professional and private life.

Spiritual Journals

The spirit has always been of great interest to the writer of journal and diary. What else is as personal and individual as one's

spiritual nature, and what form of writing more perfectly corresponds to the description of it as a journal or diary? The following are a few of these journals "of the spirit" which I have
enjoyed the most.

Gerard Manley Hopkins kept diaries when he was in his twen-
ties as an outlet for poetic expression which was still in its for-
mative stage. For him the spirit and the word were one, and
these journals show the religious side of his nature. Hopkins'
journals were the hatching ground for his poetry and are filled
with innovative word associations and juxtapositions that describe his view of God's natural world. Once he became com-
fortably fluent as a poet he stopped his journal writing; his
journals had done their work and his writing continued in the
form of poetry.

Angelo Roncalli—Pope John XXIII—kept journals which
were both a record of his spiritual path and a written account
of the battleground on which he fought his most virulent en-
emy—Pride. His journals provided him with a means of counter
attack in conquering the skepticism within himself, and they are
proof of his living faith in the structure of the Catholic church.

Thomas Merton took vows of monastic silence, but never
stopped writing. *The Seven Story Mountain* and his many books
and journals cover not only his own life, but extensive exploration into the spiritual experience, especially as manifested in
the Catholic faith.

Ralph Waldo Emerson and Henry David Thoreau, American
writers of the nineteenth century, on a more pragmatic level,
sought connection to their spirituality in nature and self rather
than in what they considered the constraints of formal religious
thought and system. They went inside in their journals to find
themselves and their own road to "enlightenment." In their public life they attempted to put this enlightenment to work.

William James, at around the same time, wrote in his *Varieties
of Religious Experience*, a highly personal interpretation of his own

belief system and his views on the place and power of organized religion in the spiritual life. He attempted to understand and interpret a 'collective' spirituality through exploring his own spiritual nature. He felt that redemption and all "cure" must come from the spirit.

C.S. Lewis, after a battle with loss of faith that accompanied the death of his wife Joy (which he documented in A Grief Observed) went on to write several books on his conception of faith. They are all personal books based on his own experience of acts of faith and the mystery of Grace.

The choices I have made of journal and diary writers are based on personal interest and preference, plus the writer's historical significance or literary importance. One is drawn in a way that conforms with one's own inner nature to a form of writing which is itself 'inner.' I have tried to give a brief overview of some of the possibilities in this genre of writing which has been such an important outlet for self-expression over the centuries. We need to go into our interior selves, and a journal is one of the best ways in which we can express what we find on these journeys. Meister Eckhart expresses it well and in great simplicity:

> *"Whatever*
> *I want to express in its truest meaning*
> *Must emerge from within me*
> *And pass through an inner form.*
> *It cannot*
> *Come from outside to the inside*
> *But must emerge from within."*

In *Walden*, Thoreau wrote:

> *"I went to the woods because I wished to live*
> *deliberately, to front only the essential facts of life, and*

see if I could not learn what it had to teach and not,
when I came to die, discover that I had not lived."

One must enter the woods if one is to ever, like Dante, exit from one's darkness into enlightenment. If we are not to end our lives in regret for parts of ourselves left unexplored we need the completion of self-examination. Journals help us to see "the essential facts of life."

WHAT DO WE NEED TO KNOW?

"There is no place you ever knew me . . .
These are not the roads
You knew me by."
Adrienne Rich, "An Atlas of the Difficult World"

"Asleep or waking
Where have you seen yourself
Mirrored completely?"

Rumi, "Fragments"

That knowledge and wisdom are part of both human need and potential is a given tenet of the human condition. We are wired to learn, to explore and to attempt to create a few finite certainties in the vast nebulae that is the unknown we are born into. Then come the questions: What do we need to know? Where does knowledge come from? What is necessary knowledge, and how do we obtain it?

There are two kinds of knowledge that make up human inquiry. One is knowledge arising from introspection—self-knowledge. The other is "external" or "public" knowledge, communal or historical in nature, which we gain through experience and the collection of evidence.

Self-knowledge must be the starting point, without it we have no other life. It is the basis of all success in the outside world. If we do not know ourselves we will find it difficult, if not impossible, to pursue external knowledge with any success. If we are true to ourselves we will intuitively and instinctively be guided to the necessary external information we should have. There is no point in trying to be another Einstein when one is meant to be a carpenter. To try to do so will end in defeat and frustration and a split in the integration of self and ego. What we are drawn to, if we listen to our *self* is a reflection of who we actually are. The beginning of wisdom is intuition.

A journal is an excellent place to tap into intuition. Intuition is notoriously elusive and difficult to either define or grab hold of. It needs to be approached with reverence, to be accessed in stillness and peace of mind. Unless we are clinically certified sociopaths we know right from wrong, and if we bother to listen we can also know if our internal and external lives are in harmony.

When we were growing up my sister had a passion for horses, I one for dogs. Since we lived in a New York City apartment I was the lucky one, my passion could, with parental reluctance, be appeased. My sister's stayed a dream until she could escape into her own life. She still has a special delight in horses, and I still need to have a dog in my life. Why wasn't it the other way around? Why was it at all? I have a compelling affinity for the Middle Ages, the period fascinates me, but American history bores me. Why? To a degree the why is unanswerable. But writing in my journal, as I studied the Middle Ages, allowed me to see the connecting links between my inside self and the outside. It is a period in history that I find in harmony with certain spiritual needs of wholeness and a defined universe that I harbor within myself. Learning about medieval history and literature is "necessary knowledge" for me because it reflects and adds dimension to my own image of reality. It may even lead to a degree of wisdom, but that these studies give me great pleasure is enough.

We oversee our own reality when we map our internal and external worlds in creative activity. Journal, memoir and autobiography lend themselves especially well to this goal-oriented mapping. Most authors start writing about themselves with a specific need they want to address, and at the heart of the question is: "What do I need to know?" "How will answers affect my life?" If the writing is to be of any benefit it must be combined with the courage to receive answers which will inevitably come from questions asked. The reason for daring to ask is simply that wholeness has become necessary, and the missing pieces, whatever they may be, must be put into place.

Following are a few quotations from authors of established or recently published books of autobiography, memoir and journal that I think attempt to answer the question, "What do I need to know?" They hold the answers of why the authors wrote their books and what they considered "necessary knowledge" to be gained by writing. We write not only in response to the question "What do I need to know?" but also because sometimes it is the only way to maintain our sense of identity. The order in which I present these books is random; there is no best or less good among them. They are all answers in their own ways. They refer in this context to the question "What do I need to know?"

In her book *The Beginning of the Journey*, Diana Trilling is very specific as to why she is writing this autobiography/biography of her and her husband, the esteemed critic, Lionel Trilling. "In addition to the pleasure of reviewing one's own life . . ." she wanted to add dimensionality to a view widely held that she thought unduly emphasized her husband's "grace and moderation." She writes:

> *"There was indeed grace in Lionel's conduct of his life. His was a moderate temperament. But these are not the qualities for which he would have most wished to be remembered. They have little bearing on the nature of his thought and speak not at all to his essentially tragic view of life. There were many contradictions in Lionel's*

personality which were perhaps not readily visible in the
classroom or in casual social encounter. It is my hope
that with the publication of this book he will no longer
be seen so narrowly."

Another reason for her writing the book was her "wish to attach autobiography to the biography of my husband." She wanted the truth and true connection of their long, fruitful and happy marriage to be recorded. Their lives were inextricably intertwined in private and professional domains, and it is appropriate their personal histories should be combined. That she outlived by many years the husband she loved and the culture they were an integral part of combined for a terrible loneliness and longing which she elegantly expresses: "Seventeen years have now passed since Lionel's death, and hour by hour, minute by minute, I still listen for a clock which no longer ticks." The longing remained, but Trilling could have the satisfaction of knowing that their "uneventful lives" had not only been lived together, but been faithfully recorded together. They were fortunate that their character and disposition met so felicitously with the reality of their public careers. This public testament to their relationship was her "necessary knowledge."

The Cloister Walk by Kathleen Norris is a beautifully written book by a poet whose writing is so closely intertwined with her spiritual life that the woof and weave of the two cannot be distinguished. It is a book about her life as a Benedictine oblate, a lay person who follows the rules of a religious order to the extent that his or her life will allow. For Norris, becoming an oblate required finding a harmonious and workable relationship between monastery and marriage—which she did. It was also a recognition that, for her, being a writer "was in essence a religious quest." Taking the vows of oblate was a formal union of the external and internal workings of her life so that they would, in conjunction, allow her to be her completed self. The book tells of the joys and benefits of the liturgical schedule and routines she immersed herself in during her monastic life. She received an unexpected gift in combining writing, marriage and a monastic life; "One pleasant surprise for me in writing this book is the way that my marriage came to weave in and out of it." There was a unity in her day's activities which changed her sense of time. The result was an end to frenzy, to wanting uncertain rewards, and to anxiety over outcome. She writes:

> *"Gradually my perspective on time had changed. In our culture, time can seem like an enemy; it chews up and spits us out with appalling ease. But the monastic perspective welcomes time as a gift from God, and seeks to put it to good use rather than allowing us to be used up by it. A friend who was educated by the Benedictines has told me that she owes to them her sanity with regard to time."*

"Sanity with regard to time" is something sorely lacking in our rushed world of instantaneous gratification and empty 'communication.' We have lost all sense of time that allows us to accomplish everything we need to accomplish. *If* we listen to ourselves, *if* we slow down, *if* we take time for time to unfold, *then* the rushing can stop.

"Liturgical time is essentially poetic time, oriented toward process rather than productivity, willing to wait attentively in stillness rather than always pushing to 'get the job done.'" Living the monastic schedule, incorporating it into her 'real life,' doing what she knew in her heart she had to do, and re-creating her experience in this book, were all part of Kathleen Norris' "necessary knowledge." The word has always been important to Norris—it was carved into her soul when she arrived on her own

"cloud of glory," and she inspires her reader with her passion in
the many quotations she weaves into her text. It is a 'journey'
book we could all read to our benefit and pleasure. It may even
transport some readers, if briefly, into Benedictine time.

In *Ghost of a Chance,* Peter Duchin has taken the fragments of
his life, tracked down missing parts and written a mid-life memoir which has allowed him to put himself together both historically and spiritually. Many of the missing pieces in the
documentary of his life were bits of information destroyed or
kept from him in the interest of his own well-being and in the
interests of the prominent families, natural and adopted, who
raised him. It is a story which backtracks from present to past,
from fact to feeling as he reworks the fabric of his life. It is a
book about memory and the nostalgia of love as well as a description of the detective work involved in finding the truth. In
a reading from his book which I attended, Duchin said his wife,
Brooke Hayward, mandated the writing as a means of clarification so that the therapy of writing could sort out fact and fiction.
She had done the same exercise in self-exposure in her own book
Haywire; the process seems to have worked for both of them.

At the end of the book, Duchin receives the first photograph
he had ever seen of his mother, himself and his father in the
hospital after she gave birth to him, before her untimely death.
It seemed to be the final piece of the puzzle, and his last sentence reads:

> "A strange calm came over me. I could see him
> sitting at the keyboard in his white tie and tails, smiling
> his broad smile. The rest of the guys were out on their
> cigarette break, and Dad was taking requests. The ladies
> had rushed to the piano, where they were gathered like
> butterflies to call out tunes. I could even see my mother
> standing behind him, lightly touching his shoulder. Pretty
> soon the dance floor would fill up."

Memory and scattered fragments of Duchin's personal history had come together, and with it the "strange calm" that accompanies self-knowledge.

My Old Man and the Sea, by David and Daniel Hays, is a journal record of a father-and-son voyage around Cape Horn. Not only is the story told in two voices, but it is told from two different perspectives. The trip was experienced and written in ways which were pertinent to the age and character of each narrator.

Daniel, the son, wanted "to find a direction for his life" and was a born sailor who seized on the opportunity for adventure. When his father read him a passage from Warwich C. Tompkins, ("There Nature has arranged trials and tribulations so ingeniously that in the van of all synonyms for sea cruelty and hardship is the ironbound name of Cape Horn."), Dan's response was, "Let's go."

For David, the father, the trip was one of reconciliation in which his mind backtracked to his deceased father and forwarded into what his own role as father should be.

The book is a wonderful sea tale; it is also a portrait of the ages of man—a reflection of how the same experience can change meaning with age. Daniel writes:

> *"We're balancing on a tightrope. On one side is our love as father and son, on the other is the way we work as a grown up team. And the tightrope, woven from a web of all the things that have happened, holds us up. Partly it's the past and partly it's love, and partly it's keeping Sparrow going fast and safely; now that has to be the most unbreakable strand."*

Of his grandfather he continues:

"This memory is special because it is all I have
of my dad's dad, yet I imagine I know him deeply
because I can see that he was close to—perhaps better to
say—he was my father the same way I am my father.
That is, we are all together in each of us."

The subject of where fatherhood starts and ends and how it connects the generations is one of David's primary concerns and something he comes to terms with in the course of their journey. There is male bonding and even some age-related male rivalry aboard the *Sparrow* as well as a deepening father-son relationship. The skein unravelled by Daniel is the more tangled of the two interwoven threads of this shared story. Either because of age or talent, or the combination of both, his narrative is more expressive than that of his father. He is more introspective, he can more easily identify his feelings and relate them to events in his life. That facility of relating to one's emotions may also be a generational attribute, as we seem to be moving away from the constraints upon expression which were a great deal stronger in previous generations than they are now.

The specter of mortality looms large for both father and son. Daniel is concerned about his father's increasing forgetfulness, he worries about the possibility that he may soon die, and he tries to reconcile himself to the sure knowledge that his father will die one day. David has a more bravura approach, it will not happen yet, but if death comes, what better place than on the high sea. When Daniel's shipboard cat dies he sums up his global concern with terminal loss in an all-inclusive, anger-filled statement: "Mortality sucks."

At the end of the trip David can state his reason for the Cape Horn trip; "I've loved sailing so much I thought I owed something back to the ocean," and he knows just as succinctly what he learned from the voyage; "The speaker is no longer my father.

It is my son." In allowing his son to captain *Sparrow*, part of his father's hold on him had been transferred to his son, the grandson.

Daniel is left with questions hanging in the salted sea air as he sails his solitary last jaunt of the journey home:

> *"Can I keep this dream going forever and never again face the consequences of human interaction? Where do I fit in and what do I do now? Am I still in my dad's shadow or can I go forward with this lead? Do I have my own permission? When will I know?"*

At Daniel's age, not everything can be immediately clarified, but the questioning is vital; the answers became his "necessary knowledge."

David did a lot more than "raise my personal and professional threshold for bullshit," one of his professed aims in taking the life-threatening trip. He answered his own nagging questions about the nature of fatherhood. That was his "necessary knowledge." They both took the journey they had to, in the same boat, looking at the same horizons appearing and disappearing over an empty ocean, but what they saw in their mind's eye, as it must always be, was an individual and shared vision for both of them. They dared a voyage that exposed their souls—what else is there in the middle of an endless ocean?

> *"We Sioux believe that there is something within us that controls us, something like a second person. We call it Nagi, what other people call soul, spirit, or essence."*
>
> Lame Deer, *Lame Deer Seeking Visions*

Practical Uses of Journal Writing

"Knowledge, if it does not determine action, is dead to us."

Plotinus, *Enneads*

Any place along the spectrum of emotion can be the catalyst for writing. We are struck at odd moments by the need to understand or express what is happening in our lives, turning points we feel compelled to examine before taking the next step on our way. There are decade markers, the 20's, 30's, 40's and on up, that cause reflection and often panic at how fast our lives are flashing by. We change jobs and careers, fall in and out of love. A new job, a move, and the parameters of marriage and family can shift and need re-defining. Death and disease cause shifting alignments which change our lives dramatically. During these times of re-calibrating balances we need to examine ourselves.

This is best done in privacy and with freedom of expression. There is no better place, and no equivalent to journal writing for self-examination. These times of change demand the presence of a whole person, and only by bringing the creative self into the picture do we become complete. We cannot go on external signs and stimuli alone. Inside is where the true signals mark our individual realities, and we cannot become complete without bringing them into cognizance.

Before the era of officially recognized psychotherapy, men and women devised their own sounding boards and became their own analysts. Their sounding boards were their creative selves; they used music, art, writing, whatever medium they were drawn to in which they could discover the universal in their own lives. Of all media of self-expression available to us today, writing is the most accessible and perhaps the least threatening.

Writing in some form is a daily experience for most people. To move from the pedestrian to a more personal form of writing is not a great hurdle to jump. To go out and purchase a set of oil paints or watercolors and easel and set up even a small studio is a major undertaking. To pursue the creative side of music is a heavy investment requiring training, practice and an understanding of the mathematical underpinnings of musical notation. Writing is a form of self-expression which comes so automatically to most of the educated world that extending it into its creative side from its utilitarian function is not a major leap to new frontiers. Writing is an accessible form of creative self-identification.

Before the age of psychologists, computers, and E-mail, a wide variety of literary traditions served the function of listener, confidante and counselor. For centuries, letter writing was the primary way in which people both expressed themselves and connected to other people and the world around themselves. Some of the most beautiful writing in any language can be found in private letters which reveal the human heart in its most intimate moments. This easy relationship with the written word spilled over into journals and diaries which were a given part of daily expression.

None of this holds true any longer. We are in a different time zone, one in which rush, not time, has taken over, and we no longer do the slow, contemplative, creative activities we used to automatically incorporate into our days. Without letters we lack connection to someone who will listen and know us and write back with advice, commiseration and the joy or sorrow which will correspond to our needs. Now we make appointments, rush to schedule one more thing into our days, and pay a stranger to do the listening, comforting and advising that should be the gifts of a connected friendship.

The pendulum may be swinging back as we approach the twenty-first century. There is a noticeable increase in the publication of books in the form of diary and memoir, collections of letters, and biographies which rely on journals and personal writing. It would seem we are ready to go inside again. The reason behind this surge of inward-looking books is not only the need to understand one's own life, but a need to be publicly known for who one really is. There is the equation that knowing will equal healing at work in all of these books. This equation is the working basis of cognitive therapy.

Of all the many forms of therapy which have hit the marketplace over the past few decades, cognitive therapy has seemed to hold up the best. Deep and lengthy analysis is expensive and time-consuming, and the results can be disappointing. Many therapists and their clients today are unwilling to undertake it. However, brief therapy is in, probably to stay, and the cognitive approach to counseling is one of its basic tenets. The simplified and basic rule of cognitive therapy is if you know something, you can change your behavior and your response to that something.

The ramifications of this simple-sounding idea have been vast, and there are heartening examples of the most ancient of dictums, "know thyself," being put to use to change and improve our lives. Self-help books can actually work and have made great impact on the daily lives and attitudes of the men and women following their precepts.

One such book which is written in the form of a daily re-
minder-cum-journal of small things and thoughts one can add
to life to make it more rewarding is *Simple Abundance, A Daybook
of Comfort and Joy*, by Sarah Ban Breathnack. Ms. Breathnack asks
her readers to shift their focus from one of servitude to one of
gratitude. Daily chores and small domestic doings can be seen
either as an affliction or as a benediction. She views daily life as
the latter, and has convinced many a tired and griping housewife
to end her day with a list of five things she is grateful for in that
day. This gratitude cancels out any anger or resentment the day
may have wrought, and it is not difficult for the majority of her
readers to come up with five items for their gratitude list. Anyone who thinks differently has only to pick up *The New York
Times* or any other major newspaper to be convinced that having
a roof over their head, bread on the table and a sane and healthy
child in bed is not to be taken for granted.

These rewards warrant gratitude. This reversal of pessimistic
to optimistic thinking is an offshoot of the cognitive approach
to mental health, and Ms. Breathnack has made it work through
writing. When one sees a list of blessings written out in their
own hand, the product of their own life, it is difficult not to be
grateful. Writing is no small delight and it brings blessings to
those who will take even five minutes at the end of the day to
sit down with their journal or notebook and write. Writing
works miracles on anger and can turn it into a creative source
of energy.

I have discussed journal writing as a therapeutic tool with
many psychologists, and have found most of them use it as a
means of understanding their client's problems—and finding solutions. Abraham H. Maslow, the psychiatrist famous for making
the expressions "peak experience" and "self-actualization" part of
our psychological vocabulary, has written a great deal that can
be applied to the act of creative writing. In his book, *Toward a
Psychology of Being*, he identifies the fear I discussed at the begin-

ning of this book that keeps so many people from undertaking journal writing. It is the fear of knowing who we actually are, of exploring all of our potential, because once we recognize the possibilities open to us we know we will have to act on this knowledge. "We must realize not only that they try to realize themselves, but that they are also reluctant or afraid or unable to do so."

Maslow is a firm believer in the merits of self-knowledge, but he also admits that it is one of the hardest tasks we ever have to undertake:

> *"Self-knowledge seems to be the major path of self-improvement, though not the only one . . . Self-knowledge and self-improvement is very difficult for most people. It usually needs great courage and long struggle."*

He neatly presents his 'summa' of human endeavor and the meaning of existence when he writes:

> *"The group of thinkers who have been working with self-actualization, with self, with authentic humaness, etc., have pretty firmly established their case that man has a tendency to realize himself. By implication he is exhorted to be true to his own nature, to trust himself, to be authentic, spontaneous, honestly expressive, to look for the sources of his action in his own deep inner nature."*

Everything Maslow exhorts us to do in order to become our real selves can be done in journal writing.

As an extension of journal writing psychologists often treat difficult problems through letter writing. The client will be asked to write a letter to the husband she has lost and resents, the father who molested her whom she still fears, the boss who is taking a young family's time together, the CEO whose decisions have forced an early retirement and caused impotence—the list of situations is endless. The client is asked to read his or her letter and imagine the person they writing to is present. In the honest and open telling of the situation, clarified in writing, lies healing.

When an alcoholic or addict is out of control, often a confrontation known as an "intervention" is chosen as a brutal, but effective, means of getting through to a numbed soul in need of help. A small group of close family members and friends writes letters explaining the reasons why they can no longer tolerate the person's behavior. If the loved one continues to drink or take drugs each person involved may have to take a drastic action in their loved one's best interest and in order to take care of *themselves*. It is often a harsh ultimatum, but one which always includes a fervent declaration of love and caring for the person who is hell-bent on self-destruction.

The letters which are the crux of this intervention are carefully written, meticulously considered and often re-written because what they say may be potentially life-saving. These missiles always come from the deepest part of the human heart and they are about love. It takes time to write them, a great deal is at stake, and almost always the person on the receiving end is deeply affected, and deeply hurt, but also touched by the knowledge that they are loved. Sometimes it works, sometimes it does not. It is always worth the try.

Writing as therapy is used in many ways, some more extreme than others. A radical approach is occasionally required. A friend of mine who was suffering from depression was asked by her therapist to set her alarm and get up at 4:00 a.m. and write her thoughts and feelings in a journal. She could write anything that came to mind, just as long as she wrote.

My friend was living in rural New Hampshire, and it was midwinter, a New England winter which is brutally cold and dark and conducive to hibernation. The last thing anyone, let alone a person in the throes of depression, wants to do in these winters is to get up in the freezing pitch black, turn on the lights and pull oneself out of a dazed sleep to write. But she did. She wrote, she wept, she returned to a deep sleep and woke at her regular waking time feeling released and rested as if she had slept the sleep of Rip Van Winkle. After the first week of this routine, her ability to cope with her daily life improved. After a few months her depression had lifted and she was able to get on with a healthy functioning life.

The physical act of writing purged toxic thoughts, lightening the writer's spirit and enlightening her mind. It was hard, cold and uncomfortable work, but it achieved its goal—release from depression. Although D.W. Winnicott, quoted earlier, has helpful things to say about depression, it is not a state of mind anyone wants to be in—the sooner out of it the better. He considers depression a part of wholeness and sees its merits as part of the larger, complete picture of self we must own up to. It is "the price to be paid for integration."

> "... health that is inherent in the capacity to be
> depressed, and the depressed mood being near to the
> ability to feel responsible, to feel guilty, to feel grief, and
> to feel the full joy when things go well. It is true,
> however, that depression, however terrible, is to be
> respected as evidence of personal integration."

Depression is a form of integration we would rather bypass, but perhaps a necessary time in the totality of our experience.

In journal writing a form of cognitive therapy automatically takes place as we see our actions and reactions recorded on paper, in words, with a reality that the actions themselves in transience often fail to convey. Once we have put an act or an idea into words it becomes real. In this act of recognition it becomes something we have some control over. With our own words in front of us it becomes easier to outline what we would like to change, what is possible to change, and what for the moment remains unchangeable, but perhaps is more bearable for being known out in the open of one's journal.

Journals make our lives present, and accessible to us. It is the unknown that defeats us. The only unknown which is not defeating, is the ineffable unknown which is faith, and that lies far above and beyond cognitive information. Much of good therapy lies in asking the right questions, and in keeping a journal we find ourselves asking them. It works. It is a solid and proven system of self-help which is used by many professionals in the mental health field. It is one we can all use constructively at home, alone or in conjunction with therapy.

In the chapter on writing exercises I used the example of what a student of mine chose to write about. When she began her journal she had no idea why she was so miserable. She knew she felt unhappy in that vanishing state where one is disconnected from herself. She did not know why or how to regain her self. In her writing she began to see ghosts appear and take shape. She realized that members of her family were playing out roles different from what she had thought them to be. She started to draw parameters to her life, and in doing so emerged from the shadows and became real again. She needed to clarify her life, and she was able to through her writing. This is an option which is open to anyone who will make the effort to sit down and examine their life in a journal.

The challenges we face require close examination if we wish to learn from them. Few of us get by with just the normal challenges of change and growth and moving on, we usually have to weather at least one real storm that makes a lighthouse necessary for survival. During these storms a journal can be a light-house—a beacon—showing us the way home. Paradoxically, often the only way to avoid shipwreck is by living in the heart of the storm, staying with it, and describing it in all its fury. We need to be in the storm to understand it, then re-create it in some form that allows us to incorporate the experience and finally be released from it.

A student of mine who had lost a child to a freak automobile accident was filled with deadly hatred for the driver of the car that had blindly swerved out of a side street. She was consumed by her anger and resentment, the energy of which, unvented, would have destroyed her. Not knowing what else to do, she wrote, and kept writing. All her anger, all her loss, all the memories and love of twenty-two years churned out day after day, night after sleepless night. She wore herself out, but she did not kill the driver of the car, and bit by bit the hatred washed away and she found herself writing about love, about the too-short life she had shared with her son. Then the intensity of love took over from the intensity of hatred and she began to come back to herself, a changed self, but herself nonetheless.

I have had students who have received the news of severe illness as a gift. For them, it was a chance to take control of a situation that would irrevocably change their lives and turn it into a life-enhancing experience that would become part of their wholeness. The only way one can make adversity a gift is to examine it, know it, and incorporate it into the newly emergent person who is the survivor. They depended on their journals as means of seeing manifested the experience of their illness. They made the discovery that illness connects in as many ways as it disconnects. There is a camaraderie among the sick which elicits understanding and compassion. All of these are emotions that we tend to forget exist in our rushed, healthy days. Illness is transformative; it takes us into ourselves but also out of ourselves in ways which can be clarifying. In order to perceive the changes

that illness brings into one's life they need to be seen, examined
and re-created, all of which a journal provides for. In writing my
students took control of disaster and were able to receive the
gift of appreciation for life.

One tends to think crises provoke people to seek something
new or corrective in their lives. But good times can be as stressful
as bad ones. Without self-esteem, a component of human nature
sadly lacking in many people these days, a good life can carry
its own perverse burdens. They often provoke the questions,
Why me? What did I do to deserve this? This couldn't be for
me, it's a mistake. I have seen more people in a state of angst
over unforeseen windfalls and glorious times than I have people
who crack under the strain of painful stress. Adversity often
brings out the best in human nature; blessings seem to tow guilt
in their wake. Adrenaline kicks in when we need it in crisis.
Calling up self-esteem is harder, and guilt is difficult to get rid
of.

It took one of my students months to begin to enjoy a new
home which she could afford to purchase after her parents died.
She had the feeling she did not deserve it and lived like a spectator in her own life for those initial months, feeling the house
didn't really belong to her. She lived in a schizophrenic separation of self from self until she began to write in a journal.

We started from the beginning: she wrote about her childhood, her life with her parents, and the intense and often difficult caring for them at the end of their lives. She wrote about
love and the generosity which had been a great part of their
family life. Little by little she came to accept the house as a
continuation of her life with her parents, rather than as a fantasy
winging into her life from the blue.

The house slowly became her parents' gift to her, because
they loved her, because she had always been there for them,
because she was their daughter, and finally, because she was
supposed to have it. The acceptance did not happen overnight,

it happened in the daily slow writing of her history and exploration of feelings past and present. But there did come a summer's morning when she looked out at the garden she had planted and knew the house was home and it was where she belonged. The guilt had been written to rest, and her new life had begun.

Of all emotions that require an extra dimension to express themselves, love is the most demanding. Love takes us into an altered state, our energy level soars, we become aware of nuances we had never before noticed. The world becomes transformed and that added energy needs to find expression beyond the radius of the object of love.

The beginning of a love affair is an ideal time to indulge in one's journal. We need the added release hatch a journal provides, and love thrives on an active imagination. To explore the erotic nature of love and sexual encounters can add greatly to the enjoyment of both. And it can be marvelously done in the privacy of a journal. The desire to describe and hold close a new love is almost irresistible, it is an inbuilt need to capture and keep this new prize.

Writing offers us an ideal way in which to add imaginative dimensions to what is already a wonder-filled experience. Journals are private so the wildest thoughts can run free over its pages. Eroticism still has its taboos, and many people are not comfortable with anything but a secret exploration of this side of themselves. A journal allows for that privacy as well as providing a place where this essential side of ourselves, which we often keep hidden, can unfold.

There is a world of difference between eroticism and pornography, although I think a certain lingering puritanism often conflates the two. The erotic is an essential part of who we are; pornography is perversion of this attribute. Our erotic selves should be explored along with all the other parts that make up our whole being—it is a great deal of fun to sit down with one's journal and intentionally explore what is going on in one's erotic daydreams. Amazing things happen! It is great for love affairs!

The well known French novel, *The Story of O*, published under a psuedonym, was written by a middle-aged, dowdy French woman in an attempt, to regain her lover's flagging interest. She began the book as notes and letters to inflame his curiosity. It worked, rekindling not only his sexual interest, but his literary interest as a publisher, and she wound up with a best-seller. The book is a good example of eroticism in literature. Pornography is stultifyingly boring. Eroticism can be thrilling. Writing erotic entries in one's journal can break routines and offer revelations of depths usually submerged like the legendary island of Atlantis. It is not only a healthy outlet, but also great fun. It beats reading how-to sex books which do not touch the wellsprings of individual need, longing and desire that, when tapped creatively, show us who we are.

As a teacher of journal writing I tend to offer this friable ground as a suggestion where it seems appropriate: a marital situation which is in rocky places, or a love affair whose terrain is still an unknown wilderness. Simply knowing one can write out their erotic fantasy life can often be the "open sesame" to better communication and refreshen a stale relationship.

One of my students who had been wanting to start a journal for years, but always found an excuse to postpone it, finally gave in when she started a love affair after many years of being alone, after a devastating divorce. She was worried she might fall apart again and needed the written, evident proof of who she had become, who she was, and who she would be in the new relationship. Her writing was a validation of the durability of all the work of reconstruction she had done. She wrote in a few moments at the end of the day, just a simple jotting down of the "I did and felt such and such" today. These few moments of self-identification helped keep her from disappearing again.

One of the other parts of ourselves that we sometimes hide

is our sense of humor. There is a range of events, ideas, and observations in one's day that can trigger the reaction, "My God, this is funny!" Often these moments arrive when we are alone and there is no one to share the humor. Rather than letting the moment disappear it is possible to prolong and augment the humorous releases by writing about them. Allowing one's sense of humor to flourish is not only therapeutic, it is creative. We are meant to laugh as well as cry, and what makes us laugh is a great indicator of who we are. Keeping mirth alive in the pages of a journal is especially important for anyone living alone or with limited social contact, as writing can maintain a dimension of ourselves that otherwise might become moribund and cease to function. After a day spent alone it is wonderful to find oneself laughing over a remembered moment.

My dog used to look at me, head askew in her questioning mode, when I would erupt in laughter sitting in the kitchen at night writing my journal. She is now used to my outbursts and just raises her head in smiling acknowledgment. Havenese as a breed do smile, and they are great company for solitary laughter! Like "an apple a day," a laugh a day works wonders.

I have had more female students than men, which I used to think was a time-constraint phenomena, but now no longer do, as most women are as busy as or busier than their male counterparts. The myth of male invulnerability has by no means gone the way of the dodo bird; it is alive and lurking, a well-fed predator. Men are, I find, still uncomfortable expressing need and weakness; they continue to believe it is not "manly." Boys do not usually keep diaries; they do not lose the equivalent of their "Ophelia" selves, and they do not tend to become introspective in their middle years as many women do. But men *do* have a flourishing life of the imagination and spirit which is inside waiting to find expression. Lately there has been a rash of autobiographies by well-known men: Ben Bradley, Neil Simon, Peter Duchin, and politicians and celebrities galore. It may well be that this more formal, historical approach to their lives is more compatible to men than the looser, intimate, form of journal writing. Autobiography is a formalized, contained form of journal, and the books we are seeing now are ample proof that personal writing is not exclusively a feminine domain. It never was. Historically journals, letters and memoirs have been male territory. Except for sporadic flashes when women had their moments of power, as in the Provençal court of Eleanore of Aquitaine and nineteenth century Parisian salon life, men were the publicly creative force in "belles lettres." Gender has become androgenized to the point where these distinctions of men do and women don't have no meaning anymore. We are in the melting pot and its not likely to stop boiling away.

I have found that when men begin to explore their feelings in writing they are often capable of touching a profound spiritual response which can soon become an avid search. The world of feeling and spirit and intuition which is often denied them in their everyday life, surfaces with great vigor when they begin to explore who they truly are beyond the working, peer-acceptable facade they often have erected around themselves.

Sometimes the threat of death pushes us to the expression of our deepest thoughts and emotions. Robert Falcon Scott knew at the end of his last expedition to the South Pole that he would not survive the trek back to a safe camp. Unusually inclement weather and illness proved fatal to his scheduling. Faced with the surety of his own imminent death and, what was harder for him, the death of his expedition teammates, he assiduously kept his journal record. Near death, it becomes more than a repository for the recording of scientific data; it becomes an expression of his strong courage and indomitable faith. He writes:

"We mean to see the game through with a proper spirit . . . One can only say 'God help us!' and

plod on our weary way, cold and very miserable, though outwardly cheerful."

He describes the final moments of one of the team, Oates, who, realizing he could not go on, left the tent saying, "I am just going outside and may be some time." He did not return. Scott's last journal words were, "For God's sake look after our people." In a letter to Bill Wilson's wife, he writes of his teammate, "his mind is peaceful with the satisfaction of his faith in regarding himself as part of the great scheme of the Almighty." The reader feels that besides great courage in the face of frostbite and illness, the entire team felt they were part of this grand scheme of Providence. It was what kept the expedition going, and perhaps it was what initiated it in the beginning. Scott's journal is a factual observation of a scientific expedition—it is also a moving diary written from the heart.

Two of the most rewarding groups I have taught were men of mimimal education, 'tough guys,' construction workers, and fishermen, many of whom had not completed high school, some of whom still had problems with their adopted English language. There was not a shirker among them. Once they had decided to try journal writing they wrote every day, they were utterly honest. They accepted their awakening spiritual side, and they did not hold back—at all.

The vocabulary they used was limited, their grammar was atrocious, and their language was occasionally off the streets and off the wall—all of which was fine because they were beginning to describe themselves in ways they had never thought about, let alone given expression to. You could have cut the emotional charge and enthusiasm in our room with a knife. Not only were they opening up to themselves, but they were opening up to each other in a naked way they had never dared before. There were tears and hugs and two-cheeked Latin kisses. We became a unit, a small community, and growth was as visible as Jack's beanstalk.

The form these journals took was as varied as the men participating in class, except for the common denominator which was always the search for their spiritual side. Occasionally someone would have a problem with the idea of a journal and find another writing approach which allowed him to better express himself. One man who was completely blocked for the first three gatherings discovered letter writing. He began to write to his girlfriend and to his mother, allowing himself feelings he had never before been able to express.

The last session I always go around the room and ask people what they have gotten out of their writing and if they plan to pursue it. The answer is always that they have reached a part of themselves they did not know existed, and that yes, they planned to go on writing. I have kept in touch with some of these men. They are still writing and they are still growing. It was an extraordinary experience for me to see these 'tough' men unfold. We had fun, we laughed and cried, and we were joined in the process of becoming more complete.

Every one of us responds differently to the multitude of stimuli in our lives, and each one of us will re-create these stimuli in different ways compatible with our own natures. There are no rules that govern this blessed individuality and there should be none. What we bring to our writing is our uniqueness, that is why we do it, to find the mirror of our self without which all else is immaterial.

The basis of all creativity is intuition and listening to the intuitive voice we all have inside whether its whisper is so low we cannot distinguish it, or its bellowing so loud we flee from it in panic. It is impossible to explain intuition. The *American Heritage Dictionary* defines it as "immediate cognition . . . a perceptive insight . . . an impression . . . a sense of something not evident or deducible." In other words, intuition, like God, is ineffable. Intuition is the heart of journal writing, it is the part of ourselves that does the creative work. For intuition there are no set rules, there can only be suggestions and intimations of how it works. I could not explain how to be intuitive any more than I could explain how to get to heaven. The only truly valid suggestions to heighten one's powers of intuition, and by extension perception, are to seek a state of mind that is quiet, to be still, listen, and make room for yourself.

The word "creative" equates with unique, individual, not to be duplicated. The truly creative finds its own path, and each creative act is unlike any other. Course instructions, teachers and counselors can provide a skeleton, but they cannot constitute an entire flesh-and-blood body. The only requirement I make of my students is that if they decide to explore journal writing they write on a daily basis. What happens from there is up to acts of Grace, the Almighty, and the gifts of individuality which will make every experience of journal writing different from all others. We are like snowflakes, and snowflakes, no matter how different their course, or where they fall, have one thing in common. They are perfect. For the briefest of moments they are absolutely perfect. Journal writing, if honestly attempted may not make us perfect, but it can greatly enhance the integration of the inside self and the outside self. When the two selves meet in harmony, their notes begin to strike their proper chords. We hear their resonances, and we know they sound right and that, as Julien of Norwich and, centuries later, T.S. Eliot wrote, "all is well and all manner of things shall be well." That may be as perfect as we are likely to get.

WINTER WRITING

"Now is the winter of our discontent . . ."
William Shakespeare, *Richard III*

*I*n winter, for many of us, the outside world closes
down. Light is scarce and weak, and we feel deprived
of the variety of lusher seasons. My fish go to the bottom of the
lily pond and hibernate in near-frozen immobility until, Lazarus-
like, they surface again in the spring.

For us also winter is often a time of hibernation. Our lives
slow down and we have a chance to know once again parts of
ourselves which often remain in hiding. Winter, in its literal and
metaphorical sense, can be a time of renewing one's awareness
of the mysteries of the interior life which surface and come alive
when there are no competitive interferences. This winter life
which replaces external activity with internal awareness has a
prisonlike quality to it at times. It is no coincidence that much
soul-searching writing has been done from prison where the
writer is constrained and has only his soul's interior life as inspiration and writing as the only outlet of expression.

Imprisonment can take many forms. It can be actual confinement and separation from society for legal or political reasons; it can be the imprisonment of political or social dissent, when one has to live an underground life. Prison can be alienation from understanding, being out of touch with one's community, one's family or ultimately with oneself. An imprisoned self is analogous to the soul looking out of an ice-encrusted window onto a barren and impossibly hostile wilderness. That is when we take to writing, not only in desperation, but because in these times all interference is cleared away and we see and hear in ways which encumbered lives do not make possible. In an odd and paradoxical way imprisonment can equate with freedom and liberation of spirit as outside interference is cleared away and we are honed down to pure self. One of the reasons I am fascinated by 'prison' literature in its broadest interpretation is that it is intense, vital, and almost always an accurate reading of the reality of the person writing. In captivity, why bother to write anything but the truth? By 'imprisonment' I imply a great many conditions besides literal captivity in a cell. Writing, especially in the form of a journal or daybook often is a major link to sanity and can provide a last remaining grip on one's interior belief system. Whether one is a prisoner actually or metaphorically, writing has long been an attempt to redeem our lives from oblivion. This life-and-death writing makes fascinating reading.

Many imprisoned lives have been testaments to powers of endurance. Many of these lives have a written accounting, as imprisonment in any form demands an escape and writing of one's experience is sometimes the only exit available. Documentation of the imprisoned state is a vast subject. There are well-known political figures who have written while in prison: Ghandi and Nehru, Nelson Mandela and Jomo Kenyatta, Eamon Devalera and Vaclav Havel, to name just a few. In choosing one politically imprisoned writer to discuss I go back to the 6th century A.D., to a philosopher who had a profound influence on the centuries following his subsequent death by execution.

Anicius Manlius Severinus Boethius was the last of the Roman philosophers and the first scholastic theologian. He translated Aristotle and Plato and handed down to Medieval scholars, St. Thomas Aquinas in particular, the Aristotelian method for approaching the problem of faith. His writing was invaluable to the scholastic movement and much of it was done from prison. Boethius was accused of treason against the state and the emperor Theodoric, charged with conspiring with Justin, emperor of the east, and put to death in the year 524. While in prison he wrote his famous *Consolation of Philosophy*, a long essay on the power and beauty of reason. As Beatrice led Dante from the Inferno to Paradise, so Lady Philosophy appeared at the bedside of Boethius and led him back to reason and gifts of memory. The work is a beautiful intertwining of prose and poetry in which Boethius abandons despair and comes back to himself.

It is accessible reading. There is nothing distant about the directness with which Lady Philosophy exhorts Boethius to pull himself together. She is nothing if not practical, and begins her assessment with the diagnosis that he is in "no real danger, but suffers only from lethargy . . . He has a little forgotten his real self . . ." She reminds him, "now is the time for cure rather that complaint," and returns him to the memory of a place where he can never be a prisoner—his "native country," which is beyond any prison wall or binding chain. This is the country of self:

> "No-one who is settled within her walls and
> fortifications need ever fear the punishment of banishment;
> but whoever ceases to desire to live there has thereby
> ceased to deserve to do so."

Her cure is effected by questions probing the state of Boethius' mind, the most crucial question being "why then do you mortals

look outside for happiness when it is really to be found within
yourselves?" Continuing in this vein, she asks him:

> *"Is anything more precious to you than yourself,*
> *Nothing you will agree. If therefore you are in possession*
> *of yourself, you will possess that which you will never*
> *wish to lose, and which fortune cannot take away from*
> *you."*

But Boethius continues to bemoan his unjust fate and the ineq-
uities of fortune. His Lady Philosophy reminds him that fortune
is not constant, "she turns the wheel of change" and that the
"insatiable desire of men to a constancy quite foreign to its nature" can be their downfall. She assures the prisoner that checking the mutable laws of fortune are the constant laws of nature
and eternal law:

> *"In regular harmony*
> *The world moves through its changes,*
> *Seeds in competition with each other*
> *Are held in balance by eternal law . . .*
> *What binds all things to order,*
> *Governing earth and sea and sky,*
> *Is love."*

This theme of the conflict between mutability and constancy,
what we might now call random chaos and divine order, became
a major refrain in the poetry and philosophy of the Renaissance.
It is a conflict that can only be resolved through love, a love
equated with God, who brings order back to the universe and
makes the music of the spheres chime in sublime harmony.

This sixteenth century concept of the order of the universe
was already succinctly articulated in Boethius', *The Consolation of*
Philosophy:

"What binds all things to order,
Governing earth and sea and sky,
Is love.
If love's rein slackened
All things now held by mutual love
At once would fall to warring with each other
Striving to wreck that engine of the world
Which now they drive
In mutual trust with motion beautiful."

The philosophical and moral thoughts of Boethius expressed in the prison writing of his *Consolation* did not stop in the Renaissance; we still respect them. They have become part of the idiom of redemption. To find our way back into the light when darkness hits our lives is the most important thing we ever have to do. It is an ageless mission which echoes through the centuries. With Lady Philosophy's help Boethius wrote himself back into a state of grace and sanity: "Then was the night dispersed, and darkness left me."

Dante closes the third book of his *Divine Comedy* as he finally enters the gates of Paradise: "But then my mind was struck by light that flashed and, with this light, received what it had asked . . . the love that moves the Sun and other stars."

'Asked' may be the key word; Dante questioned and queried his way through Hell and Purgatory. Boethius was forced to answer to Lady Philosophy.

In our century William Styron ends his autobiographical book on depression, *Darkness Visible*, comparing his own ascent out of "hell's black depths" to Dante's words as he regains his vision of light: "And so we came forth, and once again beheld the stars."

There are immutable laws as well as chance fortune, and one of them is the human need to regain oneself from all forms of alienation and imprisonment. This "coming back into the light" is hard work, and as Lady Philosophy warns Boethius, we cannot afford to be "lethargic." When we are lost or imprisoned we need to question, to attempt to find the light of reason again. Writing is often the *agent provocateur* for release from whatever prison we may find ourselves in, it is one of the great illuminators when the dark shadows fall and take us from our 'real' self. Certainly this short book, *The Consolation of Philosophy*, is one of the greatest of all 'prison' journals. Boethius' notes to himself have become part of our literary and intellectual heritage.

Boethius lost his life to the executioner without regaining his freedom. That he found spiritual liberation there can be no doubt from the testament of his *Consolation*. There are other forms of imprisonment which may appear more subtle, but are no less narrowing. Any situation which causes alienation from self could be justifiably called a state of imprisonment. When we cannot be who we truly are, or if the world does not hear and understand what we are trying to say, we are in prison. Two well-known books which are journal records of this prisonlike estrangement are Anne Frank's, *The Diary of a Young Girl*, and William Shirer's, *Berlin Diary*.

Anne Frank's, *The Diary of a Young Girl* is a fascinating narrative account of a crucial period in history and a sensitively written document of a young girl's heart and soul as she moves into early womanhood; it is also the quintessence of what a journal is and why we write them. Anne Frank's Diary answers in full the question of why we write notes to ourselves. From the opening sentence we know why Anne started her journal and we also are given a strong hint of the psychological wellspring of her being. She was in the most profound sense lonely; she had no confidante who would listen to her, be there for her and help show her who she was becoming. She calls her journal Kitty and opens it with these lines: "I hope I will be able to confide everything to you, as I have never been able to confide in anyone, and I hope you will be a great source of comfort and support."

The story of Anne Frank's life is well known. She wrote her diary as a thirteen- and fourteen-year-old hiding in a secret annex with her own and several other families who were attempting to escape the Nazi persecution of Dutch Jews. She died at Bergen-Belsen three months before her sixteenth birthday. Anne was imprisoned in many ways, both literal and figurative. She literally lived in a place where she could only briefly catch a glimpse of the outside world. She was thus estranged from all the freedoms of normal life and from nature, which was for her the greatest deprivation of all. On top of the tensions inherent in a situation of too many people under extraordinary stress locked into close confinement, she felt alienated from her family, especially her mother who she found impossible to love. Part of this alienation is the natural separation of a teenager coming into her own, part seems to be an honest antipathy toward the personality of her mother. She was in many ways a prisoner of her own body, which was changing in ways too fast to keep up with, and alone in the thoughts and questionings of her emergent woman-self with no one to counsel her and no one to talk to. Her outlet was her diary, her dear Kitty, whom she anthropomorphized with an affectionate name. Anne had an amazing ability to look at herself, as if she was a spectator on her own life, and to evaluate, judge and try to change herself in an effort to become the person she wanted to be. She put no blinders on, she was honest, possessed acute powers of observation and had a sense of humor and optimism that helped balance the horrors of her existence.

The double burden of isolation from the outside world and a feeling of estrangement from her family left her lonely and deprived of vital support. She adored her father and he returned her love, but he took the side of his wife and their daughter Margot often enough to leave Anne feeling isolated. In times of familial crisis, which were frequent, she could sit down with Kitty and write: "I am seething with rage, yet I can't show it. I'd like to scream, stamp my foot, give mother a good shaking, and I don't know what else . . ." Anne wishes she could "Just once, receive encouragement from someone who loves me." Her only solace was in Kitty: "I always wind up coming back to my diary—I start and end there because Kitty's always patient." Anne suffered from the typical teenage longing and contradiction to be by herself and to be understood. She knew there are basic solutions to some of her problems, but these, especially the comfort of nature, are denied to her in her imprisonment:

> *"The best remedy for those who are frightened, lonely or unhappy is to go outside, somewhere they can be alone, alone with the sky, nature and God. For then and only then can you feel that everything is as it should be and that God wants people to be happy amid nature's beauty and simplicity . . . I firmly believe that nature can bring comfort to all who suffer."*

Unfortunately that was a comfort Anne could not know—Kitty had to take nature's place. The diary also had to be both question and answer to the newly emergent phenomena of 'love' as Anne tried to find her way through her first infatuation with Peter, the son of one of the families living in the annex and asked herself the biggest question of all: "What is love?" With all the classic "big" questions and ideas spinning in her head and finding places in her diary, Anne never lost sight of her situation and she confronted it with that greatest of all healing balms, humor:

> *"Not being able to go outside upsets me more than I can say, and I'm terrified our hiding place will be discovered and we'll be shot. That, of course, is a fairly dismal prospect."*

The refrain that beats a constant tattoo on the pages of this journal is "No one understands me." That is probably the worst imprisonment of all, but it is one Anne fights in words as she explains herself to her friend Kitty, her journal, her soul's companion. The teens under the best of circumstances are a difficult period for a young girl; under Anne's living conditions they could have been shattering. But they were not. She took her life, her thoughts, her hopes and ideals and wrote them out. She fought bravely to survive, not just on the physical level, but on the moral and psychological level where she could become and *be* all she hoped she truly was as her individual self. She was caught between the forces of good and evil which were tearing her world and her spirit apart.

> *"It's utterly impossible for me to build my life on a foundation of chaos, suffering and death. I see the world being slowly transformed into a wilderness, I hear the approaching thunder that, one day, will destroy us too, I feel the suffering of millions."*

This bleak tone is tempered by her innate optimism:

> *"And yet when I look up at the sky, I somehow feel that everything will change for the better, that this cruelty too shall end, that peace and tranquillity will return once more."*

Anne never loses track of her primary goal which is, "If only I can be myself I'll be satisfied." She has an ability to judge and correct herself which belies her young age. It is that ability, which Pamuk describes in his *The Black Book*, of being able to take a detached look at oneself. Anne writes: "It's funny, but I can sometimes see myself as others see me. I take a leisurely look at the person called Anne Frank and browse through the pages of her life as though she were a stranger." She had an amazing ability to see her own change and growth and to perceive the larger philosophical dualities of happiness and sorrow, rage and forgiveness, in both her life and the lives of those she lived so closely with. In a world fraught with evil she "ends up turning my heart inside out, the bad part on the outside and the good part on the inside, and keep trying to find a way to become what I'd like to be and what I could be if . . . if only there were no people in the world." So ends the diary of Anne Frank. In her notes to Kitty, the good, inner part of Anne came to life, flourished in her writing and remains a testament to the interior life which can bloom and even flourish in the cruelest of winters.

William Shirer's *Berlin Diary, The Journal of a Foreign Correspondent 1934-1941* is a book I first read during my freshman year at college as part of source material for a term paper on the rise of Nazism in Germany. Although that was many years ago, I still remember the overwhelming sense of frustration I got from Shirer's commentaries as he tried to tell people, both in his writing and in his broadcasts, what was happening in pre-World War II Germany. He was faced with repeated denials of a reality he knew was becoming more and more of a threat to the European community. I thought of the book then as a 'prison' journal and having recently re-read it I find I have not changed my mind.

Imprisonment takes may forms, and Shirer's prison, as is so often the case, was both physical and mental. His was one of the few voices of truth coming out of early Nazi Germany, but it bounced back unheard from ears unwilling to accept the truths of the horror which was building as Hitler put into effect his grand scheme of dominion. Shirer had to live with the schizophrenia of known truth and public refusal to recognize that truth. Personal safety for him, his wife and baby daughter was precarious as persecution became more brutal and censorship increasingly stringent. Shirer had a dangerous job, and it was a frustrating one, as he was trapped with the knowledge of a catastrophe few people were willing to recognize. His journal is fascinating reading for the historian as Shirer gives us a reading of the daily changes in political strategy and psychology of the early war years.

From the very beginning Shirer leads us into the theme and repeating refrain of his book—people are not willing to recognize what is actually happening. They try in the face of all signs to the contrary to think they can go on with their quotidian and protected lives as if nothing malevolent is going on. On April 21, Easter, 1934, he wrote: "The hotel mainly filled with Jews and we are a little surprised to see so many of them still prospering and apparently unafraid. I think they are unduly optimistic."

Again on September 9th he jots briefly "New York looks awfully good although I find most of the good people much too optimistic about European affairs. Everyone here, I find, has very positive knowledge and opinions." This blindness cut into cultural as well as political vision, although in Nazi Germany the two did go hand in glove to a large extent. Shirer notes: "Wagner's influence on Nazism, on Hitler, has never been grasped abroad." By 1937 he writes regarding new German bombings in Spain, "I feel like screaming with rage myself . . . Dr. Aschmann called us to the Foreign Office about ten a.m. to give us the news. He was very pious about it all. I was too outraged to ask questions . . . Perhaps today's action will end the force of 'nonintervention,' a trick by which Britain and France for some strange reason, are allowing Hitler and Mussolini to triumph in Spain."

But this was not the end of 'non-intervention.' And it was certainly just the beginning of Shirer's rage at a world which did not perceive what was happening to it. The frustration level was high, as he wrote from Berlin in 1937 "somehow I feel that, despite our work as reporters, there is little understanding of the Third Reich, what it is, what it is up to, where it is going, either at home or elsewhere abroad." His dispatches go from being "a little on the censured side," in 1934 to being subject to direct intervention and the cutting of his stories: "I commented 'I have seen no map of how Europe will look if Germany wins the war.' My censors held this was unfair and cut it out." The dark winter of lie and dissimulation had fallen on Europe. In 1940 his entry from Amsterdam reads: "The Dutch still lead the good life. The food they consume as to both quantity and quality . . . the things warring people never see—is fantastic. They dine and dance and go to church and skate on canals and tend their business. They are blind—oh, so blind—to the dangers that confront them."

Shirer lived in the increasingly isolated world of his knowledge, shared with a few of his co-newsmen, like Edward R. Murrow, but not shared by the politicians and general public who continued to believe and hope that all would be well. He wrote in 1939: "How completely isolated a world the German people live in. A glance at the newspapers yesterday and today reminds you of it . . . You ask, 'But the German people can't possibly believe these lies?' Then you talk to them. So many do."

There is another level of writing, besides his professional commentary, going on in this private journal. These are the notes to himself; his writing was a release from the confinement which was rapidly becoming intolerable. His journal provided an outlet for emotions that had to be suppressed on a professional level. In 1938 Shirer writes:

"The worst has happened! *Schuschnigg* is out. The Nazis are in. The *Reichswehr* is invading Austria. Hitler has broken a dozen solemn promises, pledges, treaties, and Austria is finished. Beautiful, tragic, civilized Austria! Gone. Done to death in the brief moments of an afternoon. This afternoon. Impossible to sleep, so will write. Must write something. The Nazis will not let me broadcast . . . Yet I cannot talk."

Shirer could not talk, but he could continue to write, even when it was only to himself, to express his rage and frustration and sorrow. He states in the foreword to this book that he wrote it for his "own pleasure and peace of mind," but also "with the idea that one day most of it might be published." He knew he was seeing Europe on the brink of a war that would change it forever and his profession was journalism—writing for the public. As professionally motivated and historically significant as this book is, it is also profoundly personal and one which holds the prisoner self of a wartime correspondent in its pages. At times when his professional writing was censored, Shirer wrote notes to himself. He had to. The situation was too unbearable to survive otherwise. We sense Shirer the man in entries like the one of October 8, 1939:

> "How dim in memory the time when there was peace. That world ended, and for me, on the whole, despite its faults, its injustices, its inequalities, it was a good one. I came of age in that one, and the life it gave was free, civilized, deepening, full of minor tragedy and joy and work and leisure, new lands, new faces and rarely commonplace and never without hope.
> "And now darkness. A new world. Black-out, bombs, slaughter. Now the night and the shrieks and barbarism."

A great part of the darkness was the failure to either understand Nazism or want to know the consequence once it became obviously manifest. Blindness on such a scale produced stupefaction; "Marchal Petain has asked for an armistice! The Parisians, already dazed by all that has happened, can scarcely believe it. Nor can the rest of us."

In the last entry of the journal, dated December 13, 1941, Shirer leaves a Europe brutally changed from the one in which he had come to adulthood, years that "had had meaning and borne hope until the war came and the Nazi blight."

All three of these writers, Boethius in the sixth century, and Anne Frank and William Shirer in the twentieth, found writing an essential counterattack against the isolation and confinement of their respective 'prison' situations. They lived through the winter of their spirit, bearing witness to chaos and the destruction of life as they had known and loved it. In their journals they left testaments to the power of survival and the force of creative effort to restore and guard that which is most essential to our being—the truth. Winters of discontent and prisons breed their own special rewards, they have a part in the grand scheme, if we can rise to meet them and brave this greatest test to our humanity.

Further Examples of Journals and Memoirs

"The success or failure of a man's spiritual life depends on the clarity with which he is able to see and judge the motives of his moral acts. To use a term canonized by ascetic tradition, the first step to sanctity is self-knowledge. It is the function of reason to judge these motives, to try the purity of our intentions, and to evaluate the objects of our desire and all the circumstances that surround our moral activity."

Thomas Merton, *The Ascent to Truth*

Reason sheds its light on our minds and hearts when we write and allows us to learn and judge and become morally responsible. We often imprison ourselves. We can create in our own minds the bars that keep us from freedom when we let our thoughts churn in half truths undefined and unacknowledged. There is a world of difference between an idea imagined and one visually perceived in writing. Often our minds get caught up in a circuitry run amok in mind games. Sometimes we honestly think we are being truthful when we are actually spinning a web of fabrication that enmeshes us tighter and tighter in fiction rather than reality. Then we are in prison as surely as Boethius, Anne Frank or William Shirer. When that happens, journal writing can be a way out. Thoughts in writing come out of the shadows; we can see them for what they are; the penumbra lightens as truth is revealed in the written word. By their nature diaries are honest; there is no reason to write notes to ourselves if we are not seeking honest answers and truthfully telling the tale of our lives in our daily entries. Day-books have no other purpose but to be honest, and they can release us from bonds and take us out of our fabricated prisons. A journal reminds us of the interior life that is truly who we are. Journals work both ways, they can take us inward or outward depending on the need.

Thomas Merton's life was a good example of an examined life made manifest and clarified in writing. His words still create an echo of response in their reading. Writing is one of the most accessible means we have for self-examination and self-expression, two essential functions of a complete and fulfilled life. But writing is fast slipping into disuse in this day of audio-visual communication. I do not think we can afford to let this most precious gift become an obsolete appendage.

The quotes I have used in this text come from books I have not only enjoyed, but that have reinforced my belief in the power of the written word as a creative tool. They express a basic need, the need to understand our place in the human con-dition—its joys and sorrows, humor and grief, outrage and ac-ceptance. Philosophers and scientists, rock stars and politicians, movie stars and 'sages,' from the holy to the ungodly—people seem more than ever to feel the need to explore their souls and their lives in writing. It is a confrontation with ourselves that carries with it invaluable healing, and is often called forth by need or despair. Books describing addiction and depression have transformed both phenomena from hidden taboos into illnesses that can be treated. Both are diseases of spiritual blindness and absence of faith, in which one loses sight of their soul. Writing breaks through the debilitating inertia these illnesses cause and allows one to fight back. This taking control of one's life can be a lifeline to recovery.

Loss through death also requires a catharsis which writing helps to take place. Isabel Allende's book, *Paula*, written when her daughter was dying is testament to this need for expiation in the face of intolerable loss. Journals which erupt with an author's joy in life take us into that "wonder and awe" which both Albert Einstein and Dag Hammarskjöld felt was a crucial reaction to a life fully lived. Books on gardening and crafts share with the reader the insight that comes when one gets a glimpse of the master plan and knows they are part of it. In travel memoirs, readers can know places they will never physically explore themselves. It is lovely to sit warm and comfortable and have an arduous trip to the outer reaches of some inaccessible place described to us. None of us can lead all the lives we would like to, but we can read about them. Some of the following excerpts are about places I will never see, but now feel I have known. Others tell better than I can, experiences I have known well.

People write not only to know themselves, but to be known. Writing is a double faceted art. In writing we can see who we really are, and at the same time we allow ourselves to become visible, seen and known. We actually materialize, become present and completed in the written images of ourselves. Writing allows us to receive the grace of self, that identification which describes who we are.

When children, usually girls, who tend to be more needfully introspective than boys, start their diaries it is not only an exploration of their secret selves and secret mysteries, their diaries are also a means of marking their individuality. It says this is who I am, apart from my parents, separate from the society that has raised me, this is the me that I am becoming. These children are becoming the person they want seen, manifested, and known.

Being known is a basic human requirement. We cannot exist in a limbo without identification. That would be as unnatural as being born without a set of fingerprints. When people seek psychological counseling it is often with the complaint "no one understands me"—which translates more brutally into "no one knows who I am." "I am disappearing"—is the fear behind many desperate actions. Identifying oneself in writing counteracts this fear. Even when there is no one present to affirm that "yes this is who you are," a day's entry in a journal will, in lovely concrete words, tell you, you exist, you act and react, and you are *not* disappearing. Few of us are strong enough to live without affirmation from the outside. Writing shows us our connecting links. One of the reasons I remember the opening lines of André Aciman's book *Out of Egypt* is its affirmation of being. "So are we or aren't we," "siamo o non siamo" is the oft repeated "logo" declaration of Aciman's great uncle Villi. These words act as a thematic refrain weaving its way through the pages of this lovely memoir. It is a dictum that expresses an attitude to self marked by intense individuality which was the defining trait not only of great uncle Villi, but of the entire Aciman clan. "Siamo"—We are—expresses not arrogance, but the fullness of being which was the distinguishing mark of this family. D.W. Winnicott wrote, "The central feature in human development is the arrival and secure maintenance of the stage of *I AM . . .*" Uncle Villi definitely arrived at, or was born with, the "central feature" of "I amness." We need to be known by family, friends and community, we need to know whatever it is we consider our cosmos, our universe, which is a vision of where the Almighty resides, and we need to know we can, with confidence, say I am. I think of that opening line from *Out of Egypt* and wonder to myself if I can as surely say to myself, "so are we or aren't we," knowing in my heart, like Uncle Villi, that yes I am.

Thomas Merton writes in *Thoughts in Solitude:* "We cannot find Him unless He shows Himself to us, and yet at the same time He would not have inspired us to seek Him unless we had already found Him."

God needs man as much as man needs Him. The relationship between the Almighty and us is a two-way street. There is a give and take implicit in becoming all we are meant to be. We need to seek if we are to find, and writing is one of the greatest means of seeking we possess. The list of writers who have sought, and found, redemption is long.

Anne Morrow Lindbergh in her short book *Gifts from the Sea*, touched many hearts in her search for her self which she shared in writing. She writes of a special time of discovery and renewal. She had become lost in what Zorba the Greek called, as he danced for himself on a deserted beach, "the full catastrophe." He meant family and all the responsibility, confinements and giving of self that family can demand. Lindbergh needed to retrieve her identity apart from a husband, five children and the demands of everyday life; the outer shores led to her inner beach. For lack of a beach, a journal can often serve as a separate and private place apart where we can come back to ourselves and know ourselves in the dance of writing. It is also the place in which we can converse with God and fulfill our part in the two-way dialogue which is so very crucial to wholeness. As Lindbergh writes:

> *"But I want first of all—in fact, as an end to these other desires—to be at peace with myself. I want a singleness of eye, a purity of intention, a central core to my life that will enable me to carry out these obligations and activities as well as I can. I want, in fact—to borrow from the language of saints—to live 'in grace' as much of the time as possible. I am not using this term in a strictly theological sense. By grace I mean inner harmony."*

She quite simply identifies how that special "grace" of being can be achieved. "I believe that true identity is found," as Eckhart once said, "by going into one's own ground and knowing oneself. It is found in creative activity springing from within."

In seeking redemption and inspiration we often go back to

time honored writers such as Dante, T.S. Eliot and Graham
Greene. Classics usually become so because they have something
profound to say to us. They transcend the boundaries of their
own written time and speak to every man, in every time. We go
back to them to find ourselves, in our own time, within the
totality of all time and all people. Dante is one such classic writer
and the opening lines to the first book of his *Divine Comedy* are
some of the most frequently quoted lines in the history of literature. They are worth quoting again.

> *"In the middle of the journey of our life I came
> to myself within a dark wood where the straight way
> was lost. Ah, how hard a thing it is to tell of that
> wood, savage and harsh and dense, the thought of which
> renews my fear! . . . I cannot rightly tell how I entered
> there . . . but when I had reached the foot of a hill at the
> end of that valley which had pierced my heart with fear
> I looked up and saw its shoulders already clothed with
> the beams of the planet that lead men straight on every
> road."*

T.S. Eliot's "Four Quartets" flow in and out of memory and recall
a path through past, present and future that makes all time one
seamless pattern of unending connection without beginning or
end. They inspire a process of thinking that transcends time.
Eliot's lines take us both away from and into ourselves. His writing is a celebration of the creative act of writing and his theme
of self-exploration, and the rewards of an examined life occur
again and again in his poetry:

> *"We shall not cease from exploration
> And the end of all our exploring
> Will be to arrive where we started
> And know the place for the first time."*

"Know" is probably the key word in these often quoted four lines, and knowledge is what we gain when we make the effort to explore our lives. Graham Greene's book, *Journey Without Maps*, is a journal-memoir of a trip to Africa which resulted in unexpected discoveries and unplanned re-routings. It was a trip that invented itself and mapped itself as it unfolded, as good trips always do. Greene introduces us to expectation of the unexpected from the opening paragraph of the first chapter, "The Way to Africa:"

> *"The tall black door in the narrow city street remained closed. I rang and knocked and rang again. I could not hear the bell ringing; to ring it again and again was simply an act of faith or despair, and later sitting before a hut in French Guinea, where I never meant to find myself, I remembered this first going astray, the buses passing at the corner and the pale autumn sun."*

This is an extraordinary opening paragraph. In three sentences, Greene has told us exactly where he is both physically and spiritually. He is somewhere he had not planned to be, and has "gone astray." He can react to this detour either with faith or despair. We know he is in a city, confronted by an ominously closed black door that does not open to knocking and that it is the autumn, and we know his state of mind. Description brings forth from memory the beginning of his recollected journey. Before this first chapter, Greene quotes Oliver Wendell Holmes who uses the imagery of a map to describe the human journey, a map which needs assembling and interpretation to become legible.

> *"The life of an individual is in many respects like a child's dissected map. If I could live a hundred*

*years, keeping my intelligence to the last, I feel as if I
could put the pieces together until they make a properly
connected whole. As it is, I, like all others, find a certain
number of connected fragments, and a larger number of
disjointed pieces, which I might in time, place in their
natural connection. Many of these pieces seem
fragmentary, but would in time show themselves as
essential parts of the whole. What strikes me very
forcibly is the arbitrary and as it were accidental way
in which the lines of junction appear to run irregularly
among the fragments. With every decade I find some new
pieces coming into place. Blanks which have been left in
former years find their complement among the undisturbed
fragments. If I could look back on the whole, I feel that I
should have my whole life intelligently laid out before
me . . ."*

Oliver Wendell Holmes

In our own lives we can try to put the pieces of the map in
place so that we know where we are going and from whence we
have come. Or we can stay lost. It is always the question, do
we dare, have we the strength and courage to find our way?
Greene and Holmes both answer this question in the affirmative.
They dare to both make the trip and to describe it. The alternative to answering the dare with a resounding yes is to remain
with our hearts in darkness.

When darkness has a grip on one's soul, writing can often be
the guiding light out of the abyss. William Styron, in his short
book, *Darkness Visible,* describes his own version of Hell, an abyss
of suicidal depression. During his illness he kept a notebook
whose entries were, he admitted, "erratic and haphazardly written." He planned to use this journal professionally and he also
decided that if he were to get rid of the notebook "that moment
would necessarily coincide with my decision to put an end to

myself." The moment hung in the balance for many months of struggle with his illness until finally he came out into the light of reason once more. He writes, in his own paraphrase of Dante, "For those who have dwelt in depression's dark wood, and known its inexplicable agony, their return from the abyss is not unlike the ascent of the poet, trudging upward and upward out of Hell's black depths and at last emerging into what he could newly perceive as 'the shining world.'"

Although few of us go through the demonic form of illness that William Styron suffered from, we do all have moments of despair. It is part of the human condition and inescapably woven into its complex design. If we are once more to behold "the shining world," we need all the help we can get. Journal writing is one of the greatest tools we have. When Styron was catatonic from depression he continued to write, he wrote about his illness. He took suffering and re-created it, which may well be the only way to survive it.

Susanna Kayson's book, *Girl Interrupted*, is another example of mental illness provoking a book into being. It is the story of her two year stay in Maclean Hospital in Boston, as an eighteen-year-old having serious problems growing into adulthood. It is one of the saddest and yet funniest books I know. Sad because the incarceration of a young, bright woman in an asylum is tragic, funny because she has an unrelenting and irrepressible sense of humor. Kayson describes the slip into madness in an almost lyrically analytical way that is perfectly lucid.

> *"And it is easy to slip into a parallel universe. There are so many of them: worlds of the insane, the criminal, the crippled, the dying, perhaps of the dead as well. These worlds exist alongside this world and resemble it, but are not in it . . . Another odd feature of the parallel universe is that although it is invisible from this*

side, once you are in it you can easily see the world you came from. Sometimes the world you came from looks huge and menacing, quivering like a vast pile of jelly; at other times it is miniaturized and alluring, a-spin and shining in its orbit. Either way, it can't be discounted. Every window on Alcatraz has a view of San Francisco."

Kayson created her own "room with a view" in writing about her illness—and she may have written her way back to sanity in the journal book of those hospitalized days. She describes a nurse accompanied trip with some other "inmates" to the local ice cream parlor:

> *"There were no other takers for peppermint; chocolate was a big favorite. For spring they had a new flavor, peach melba, I ordered that.*
> *'You gonna want nuts on these?' the new boy asked.*
> *We looked at one another: Should we say it? The nurses held their breath. Outside, the birds were singing.*
> *'I don't think we need them,' said Georgina."*

Kayson pricks her demons with a humor that allows her to get the upper hand. I would think humor played a great part in her recovery. Two years in a mental hospital gave Susanna Kayson a new perception of the human condition. She knew that perhaps her grip on reality would always be tenuous, but it would also be fortified by the ability to describe who she is and where she is in her life. Writing helped free her from her "Alcatraz," it was an escape route from prison.

Writing is one of the best therapies available when sanity seems questionable, or even, as in the case of Styron, impossible. Writing releases the pent-up monsters who inflate to bursting when left to themselves. These monsters usually cannot survive the light of scrutiny and observation. Like Beowolf's tormentor Grendel, they dwell in darkness. When the demons of thought are put onto paper they are tamable. We can say "Aha that's who you really are—I can do such-and-such about you and I will loosen your hold on my mind. I will not follow you into your foul cave." Then we, not they, are in control.

Good travel books are always more than a description of places visited. True travelers change on their journeys. The maps of our minds enlarge and shift, balances get re-weighed and equilibriums newly hung. Change is provocative and can be fearful. Travel diaries and memoirs help stabilize new feelings and have long been popular companions of trips made and remembered. Writing helps clarify images as we individualize our own view and make vistas seen often before our own personal descriptions. The same sun-paletted Aegean Ocean, fragmented into dazzling splendor under a hot Greek sky will connote something different to every thoughtful eye that sees its. All of us are attached to a different system of reaction which includes memory and desire, longing, and our own criteria of beauty. By describing our reactions we make a place ours, it becomes part of who we are. Again this reaction is a two-way street, since places respond to the effects they create. If a beautiful place is not seen as beautiful and treated as a treasure to be preserved and honored it will not remain lovely for long. Places lose their souls if they are not touched and do not find refrain in the souls who know and inhabit them. There is always answer and response; we cannot enjoy the world without an echo on our part.

One of the most beautifully written travel journals I have come across is Lady Lawrence's *Indian Embers*. Lawrence was a novelist, and had the skills of an accomplished writer. She writes honestly, and with great descriptive originality. She opens her journal on April 1914, upon her arrival in India as the wife of a highly placed member of the English government, which was

then still very much in control of Indian political life. She ends
her journal in March of 1919, as she and her husband are leaving
India—for good—in the face of a changed political scene that
is no longer hospitable to British help or interference.

In the five years covered in her journal many changes take
place in India, in the British-Indian political establishment, and
in her own life as a mother and a wife. Anyone contemplating
an arduous trip might do well to put a copy in their travel case.
Lawrence's spirit, fortitude, and above all humor in the face of
daunting challenges is a testimony that we can do things that,
until confronted, might have seemed impossible to us. She manages life on very civilized terms, despite the deprivation of lux-
uries to which she had been accustomed. She faces dangers from
insects and reptiles and extremely inclement weather. Lawrence's
husband was away a great deal for his work, and he was often
emotionally absent due to temperament. He had the perfect
mate for his job, one who did not complain and accompanied
him everywhere possible. Her writing was her companion in
moments of loneliness and alienation in a strange country and
it remains one of the great travel books of this century.

Lady Lawrence captures a time and place that is irretrievably
gone except in description. *Indian Embers* is among the best descriptive writing. It has the ability to "take us there." She describes a languid afternoon with her husband:

> *"Henry returns to his files, and I to my long
> chair, in a trance. The vast sky and the vast river are
> divided by one blinding line of mustard sliding by. Great
> golden Sindi boats, laden with grain, with their huge
> rudders turning this way and that, dream past with idle
> sails, and there are little fishing craft with a spidery
> circle of net, and the graceful figure of some Homana
> woman bent against the long steering pole. Here is a
> white crane on the side of a small boat, patiently fishing*

*for his master, so tight a ring around his neck he cannot
swallow his prey for himself. Glassy sky, glassy water,
hours fused in glare seem to stand motionless like
reflections in a mirror. How is it possible for Henry to
continue working so methodically?"*

Lady Lawrence also describes terrible bouts of malaria that leave
her soaking in icy sheets, every bone and muscle in her body
wracked, head exploding in pain. This is a book the reader will
return to in memory.

As well as creating new images in readers' minds, travel memoirs can also dispel preconceived and often romantic notions in
their factual detailing of a trip made or country explored. A
recently published book that had that effect on me is *Sahara
Unveiled: A Journey Across the Desert* by William Langewiesche. I
cannot remember a time when the concept of 'the desert' has
not lured me. My interest began as a fascination with caravans,
desert sheiks in their tents, notions of oriental splendor and what
I imagined as a nomadic life of intriguing decadence. This "Sheik
of Araby" vision was replaced by an image of stretching sands
that offered absolute quite, peace and a chance to touch the
spirit of God. A place where the desert fathers retreated to find
their God and their own soul. Langewiesche's book did nothing
to lessen my interest, on the contrary, but it did change my
knowledge of the reality of the desert. He is a journalist, and
his account of this trip through the Sahara is explicit and in
many ways brutal. It dispels all illusion and his opening lines
warn that this is exactly what he intends to do:

*"Do not regret the passing of the camel and the
caravan. The Sahara has changed, but it remains a
desert without compromise, the world in its extreme. There
is no place as dry and hot and hostile. There are few
places as huge and as wild."*

The desert of Langewiesche's narrative still holds places of stir-
ring beauty and offers silence and vast emptiness for prayer and
worship, but his unveiling gives his reader an actuality which is
often harsh. He asked a traveling companion why he wanted to
pray in the desert and received the response, "Because the sand
here is clean," as his friend goes off alone "to bathe his soul in
it." But the desert is also a place to die in, and Langewiesche
describes the terrible deaths of a Belgian family who became lost
and whose last days are documented in a journal kept by the
wife. In answer to his own question of why a woman would keep
a journal when she was fighting a painful battle against death he
writes, "People dying of thirst in the desert often leave a written
record. They have time to think. Writing denies the incredible
isolation." The Belgian woman's journal was truly writing in ex-
tremis, it was a last attempt to maintain a vestige of her humanity.

The genre of journal, diary, memoir is fascinating because it
can provide a true description of one person's attempt to understand his or her own particular place in a grander scheme.
There is usually an intensely personal tone in memoir which
allows the reader to feel they "know" the author. There should
be, somewhere, a revelation which says this is who I really am,
I want you to know this about me. Writing is an allée to
thoughts and emotions and a statement of what is true of one's
particular nature.

Two recently published memoirs allow their readers to feel
they know their writers heart and soul.

Barbara Grizzuti Harrison's book *An Accidental Autobiography*
weaves in and out of the memories of her sixty years of travels
and love affairs of all kinds. She is a passionate woman and
frankly states that she has a propensity to indulge in whatever
captures her interest. One of these indulgences is food. Food is
a passion with her, a need that corresponds and links into many

of the other "love affairs" of her life. It is also partly her undoing and responsible for landing her in a hospital. She makes no bones about her love of food or the consequences of too much of a good thing and writes quite simply, "I am fat." But what delights she has in her indulgences!

Harrison indicates in the introduction that memory for her is not linear, it is "a town in Italy that is made of five concentric circles" . . . and "is perfectly logical" . . . She finds it natural to weave into her life and thoughts recountings that follow her own logic.

> "Memories gather around puzzles, passions, and possessions; they shelter daydreams, which in turn give birth to memories that are new to the concious mind. Round and round we go. Memory is no more linear than it is hierachal. Synchronicity and caprice, improvisation and intransigence are the engine by which memory drives and is driven; and so is repetition, and so is contradiction, neither of which I have disavowed."

Harrison reacts strongly to her life, and writing is an integral part of her reaction. Writing is as necessary a complement to anything she does as eating is to the fabric of her days and lovers to the pleasures of her nights.

Peter Duchin, in *Ghost of a Chance*, takes a linear approach to the telling of his life. His objective in writing was different from Harrison's. He was on a quest to solve the mysteries of how he got to be who he is. Along with the descriptions of the events of his life is the Peter Duchin who lets us see who he truly is when he describes listening to Bach, or when he writes of fishing, an act he undertakes with reverence:

> "Instant gratification is not what fishing is all about. The first thing fishing does is make you slow

*down—way down. You can't be any good at it unless
you stop everything and begin to look, really look—
whether it's for terns diving into a stretch of the Gulf
stream (a sure sign of fish below) or that dimple on a
slick glacial lake (sure sign of hungry trout)."*

Memoirs can have a feeling of revision lacking in more casually recorded journals that give them a polished and sometimes distant aura, but if honesty is present, the reader can say to himself, "That's who I'm reading about." Harrison is a writer who has had great success in her chosen work. Duchin has recently found writing and has probably discovered how revelatory it can be. Both authors write as if it is as important for them to *be known,* as it is to know. Description of the outside of our lives can, as Anne Morrow Lindbergh said, "Help one to find the inside answer." This inside answer that can provide self-knowledge and the possibility of a life lived in a "state of grace" and peace with oneself.

Marianne Williamson whose book, *A Course in Miracles,* has inspired many people, writes of the need to affirm, as opposed to simply accepting belief. She writes of the need of an active response to knowledge of God's will:

*"I declare that it is His will being done—I
declare it! That is different from just knowing it. Just
knowing it is passive. Declaring it and affirming it and
stating our intention are active. This approach uses the
power of our mind to cocreate that manifestation in our
life."*

Writing is an essential response to what is happening in our lives. The alternative is a passive, uncreative, unevolving life, one in which we neither know ourselves nor let ourselves be known.

One of the nice aspects about writing is that it is a pursuit one can follow till the end of one's days. It is not a skill limited to the young and able, only the severest handicaps make writing an impossibility, and, as writers like Stephen Hawking have shown us, even the most limiting handicaps can often be overcome. Florida Scott-Maxwell's book, *The Measure of My Days*, was written when she was in her eighties, housebound and hindered by illness. When I started her journal I expected to find complaints or feelings of dislocation in a world that was changing beyond her capacity or desire to change with it. I anticipated sadness, fear, anger; emotions I associate with old age. What I did not expect to encounter was passion, accompanied by the enormous frustration of not being able to manifest that passion in her life. It had not occurred to me that passion unfulfilled would be one of the great sorrows and challenges of age. She writes: ". . . but my eighties are passionate. I am more intense as I age. To my own surprise I burst out in hot conviction."

Without a daybook to describe and release her feelings she would have been locked inside herself and that would have eaten away at her. She observed, "My notebook shows me how much I mourn." Indeed she mourned, but through her journal she expressed this sorrow so that she could live with, not against it. She took her thoughts out of her head and put them on paper where she could see the proof of who she had become, and was becoming in her final years.

> *"What matters is what I have now, what in fact I live and feel. It makes my note book my dear companion, or my undoing. I put down my sweeping opinions, prejudices, limitations, and just here the book fails me for it makes no comment. It is even my wailing wall, and when I play that grim, comforting game of noting how wrong everyone else is, my book is silent, and I listen to the stillness and I learn."*

Learning is an antidote to aging. We cannot avoid the physical changes and deterioration of the body, but we can arrest aging of the mind—by constant renewal and challenge. Scott-Maxwell's book is an intensely spiritual one, fervent with the passions of old age. Regret and longing hover over her days and sometimes sleepless nights but her writing gave her the ability to live in a state of grace with her God and herself. In an earlier quote, she describes the fealty owed to the ascension of man from unconsciousness to experiencing the spirit within himself:

> *"Can we do less than give fealty to such*
> *ascension? I do not think we can, I think we must give*
> *that fealty which is loyalty to oneself, and keep up an*
> *ongoing search for the identity within which is our soul."*

The Measure of My Days was part of her search and makes full testament to the popular phrase "old age is not for sissies."

Dag Hammarskjöld's *Markings* is an extraordinarily intense book of observation, poetry, self-critique and ultimately, a statement of faith. One feels on reading it that they have entered the very heart and soul of the writer. Hammarskjöld begins his journal in 1925. He opens it with a poem entitled "Thus it was." Its opening lines are:

> *"I am being driven forward*
> *Into an unknown land.*
> *The pass grows steeper,*
> *The air colder and sharper*
> *A wind from my unknown goal*
> *Stirs the strings*
> *Of expectation*
> *Still the question:*

Shall I ever get there?
There where life resounds,
A clear pure note
In the silence."

The journal ends in 1961 with another poem which is in many ways an answer to the first one.

"Twice I stood on its (the mountains) summits,
I stayed by its remotest lake, And followed the river
Towards its source.
The seasons have changed
And the light
And the weather
And the hour.
But it is the same land.
And I begin to know the map
And to get my bearings."

Hammarskjöld got to know the map of his own journey between 1925 and 1961 thoroughly. Through intense examination he created a route that, in the end, was true to himself and reflected his individual way. "The longest journey is the journey inwards of him who has chosen his destiny."

Hammarskjöld uses a style of writing perfectly suited to what he wants to say. He writes in short, concise paragraphs that could appear choppy if his focus were not so clear we never lose track of where he is going. Sometimes four or five lines are complete in and for themselves. One such very short tale is:

"He was a member of the crew on Columbus's
caravel—he kept wondering whether he would get back
to his home village in time to succeed the old shoemaker
before anybody else could grab the job."

That is all. And it is *everything*. A man had a chance to take a great journey, be part of an heroic adventure, to know the "quest." But he could not. He lacked vision and courage and busied himself in the pedestrian worries of daily ambition and gain. He sailed with Columbus in a voyage of discovery, but his mind stayed at home. This is equivalent to the fear that keeps many people from the discovery of writing. Hammarskjöld did not stay locked into the narrow confines of the known, he did not try to keep himself protected from the ineffable: he braved the journey.

In her recently published biography *Architect of Desire* of her great-grandfather Stanford White, Suzannah Lessard is open about how painful it was to confront her family history rather than the myth it had (over generations) become. Sexual injuries committed by White had been whitewashed by her family with destructive emotional consequences. In the writing she found truth, and in the truth she became both whole and free. She writes:

> *"We cannot therefore know ourselves truly without seeing when there is terror in harmony; without registering in our marrow a coldness that may feel like warmth, or violence that presents as lust for life. We try to see these things not to demolish but to strive toward a whole world, because an unwhole world is ghostly: no matter how beautiful it might be, no connection is possible there. We do this not to place blame but to make connection possible. We do this to live."*

Without connection a real life is impossible. If we remain like Columbus' crew member fearful of the journey we have no life.

Like Hammarskjöld and Lessard, we have to dare to see, and dare to describe what we see. These are the reasons why diaries and journals were written, it is why they continue to bear proof of our need to re-create ourselves—to know and be known.

Part III

Notes from Myself

"... he kept wondering if he would get back to his home
village in time to succeed the shoemaker."
—Dag Hammarskjöld

> *"So one cannot deny that heaven and earth are still in touch, and we can easily discern what is the real life of the spirit and what is, instead, mere appearance; we can see what is but external illusion and what is, instead, our strength and vitality."*
>
> Pope John XXIII, *Days of Devotion*

The reason I write is quite simply to maintain my belief and sure knowledge that indeed "heaven and earth are still in touch."

I have found in trying to inspire friends and students with my fervor for journal writing there is a generalized sense of paralysis among the most enthusiastic would-be writers when it comes to the moment of actually starting. In my own writing there is often the challenge of laziness, inertia and sometimes depression that can annihilate all desire to do anything. But not fear. Perhaps because I have been writing in journals for almost my entire life I have forgotten that long ago moment of trepidation. Once faced and conquered, the rest is easy. It is a few moments, a day's entry, that is all it takes to eliminate the block. Sometimes a crisis will push one into confronting their journal because there is simply no other way to bear it—or to enjoy it. Illness, beginning an irresistible but confusing love affair, moments when we need to make our way to our most interior selves will push us beyond fear to write. Then it becomes, if not easy, at least possible. Usually well beyond the illness and the love affair the writing continues. Because by then we *must* write; we feel a dimension in our lives missing without it.

Discussing journal writing at a dinner party recently, a young mother told me how she started a journal after the difficult birth of a baby who needed intense postnatal care. She had to keep track of medications, and the progress of her baby during a four-and-a-half month hospitalization. She had planned to do only that, keep her records. But she found that soon the jottings of medication and progress began to include comments on how she was feeling about the difficult and highly emotionally charged period in her life. These brief recordings of her ups and downs expanded little by little and she began spending more time on her journal, thinking about what was happening to her in the worry-fraught days and nights of her child's recovery. The journal became a reflection of this important and dramatically changing event in her life. What was happening to her child had profound effects on how she was adjusting to becoming a first time mother, a difficult enough transformation under the best of conditions. Her journal was a means of self-definition, a friendly confidante and much needed escape as well as a record of medical progress made. She does not keep a journal on a regular basis now, but she does know, from that acutely difficult time, that she can write in a journal, that this written response to events in her life helps define them, and that writing naturally evolved for her in a time of crisis. Journal writing is something she now knows she can use whenever she needs it. We are led to writing in our own ways and with our particular needs. This young mother started with recording basic facts and data, but she moved quickly beyond fact to feeling, led by the articulation writing gave to her daily challenges.

Facts are a good start for any new creative project, like Boudin's notations of wind and weather conditions in the corner of his paintings. Sorrow and joy, pain and ecstasy all are more fully part of us when they have the extra dimension of written examination. We do not need to wait for tragedy or crisis to begin to write, but sometimes these are the catalysts that show where healing may be found.

For anyone living alone or feeling moments of separation there is an added attraction to keeping a journal—seeing oneself mirrored in one's writing. Perception by another person is missing when one lives by oneself and one can feel diminished and unreal, a shadow person. Through writing one negates this disappearance of persona as the writing becomes the observer, commentator and companion to our life. In writing we gain identity and clarity that countermands the lack of response and answer in the solitary life. A journal says loud and clear, yes you are a person, you are growing and changing and this is who you are becoming. It is easy to feel that if no one hears us, our quirky joke or our profound observation, then we do not exist. If one writes there is always a response: we respond to ourselves. Living alone may be fun, but it is not funny. It is comforting to read one's journal and see that a sense of humor has not abandoned us. It is O.K. to laugh with oneself, by oneself, and above all, for oneself.

Knowing we are going to write makes us more observant. There is an added acuteness to vision when it is joined to word. When you write about what you have seen in your day you are also writing about what you are choosing to see. This indicates a great deal about your current state of mind and your emotional balance.

Perception is a reflection of feeling. And vice versa. We often blind ourselves to the things we do not want to acknowledge or that will be uncomfortable. Your writing allows you to recognize your blind spots. As in driving, blind spots can be dangerous if you do not know they are there.

Anyone who has lived through a prolonged siege of murky weather, where sun and moon remain hidden and all the signs and remonstrances of God seem to have disappeared, knows how important reflection is. Without the sun during the day and the moon at night there are no reflections. There are no shadows cast, no wavering, constantly re-defining, shifting images to fascinate the eye and mind with their play in light. There is a dimension missing and we feel the lack of it. We get depressed and frustrated, it is like living at the bottom of a well. The image of sun-less, reflectionless life is the physical equivalent to a mentally and emotionally unexamined life. We need to have the reflection of creative work to know who we are, where we have been and where we are going. Images change and shift, they are enhanced in their light-reflected images. Our souls act in the same way to the creative acts which shine back at them.

The Turkish writer Orhan Pamuk, in his novel, *The Black Book*, tells a story of a man whose persona merges and conflates to such an extent with another man that he loses track of who he is. It is a fascinating book about identity—how we find it, how we keep it, how essential it is to know who we are. At the end of the book the 'hero' writes:

> *"This 'I' that I observed as if in a dream was nobody but myself. What astonished me was the unbelievably gentle, sweet and loving affinity I felt for this person."*

Awareness of self is always the result of work done in the imaginative mind. I think it is impossible to escape feeling empty without this evolved self-awareness. James Cowan has recently published a short novel, *A Mapmaker's Dream*, which is meditation and prayer woven into the story of Fra Mauro's creation of the map of his own mind and imagination. The medieval monk stays in his protected cell and receives visitors from the farthest corners of the earth. He bemoans his own cowardice in remaining in the enclosure of his cell while his mind ventures and takes other people's risks, but that is his way and at the end of the book he acknowledges:

> *"Each of us has the right to speak of his coastline, his mountains, his deserts, none of which conforms to those of another. Individually we are obliged to make a map of our own homeland, our own field or*

meadow. We carry engraved in our hearts the map of the world as we know it."

Fra Mauro created the map of his world in his imagination and through re-working the travels and explorations of his friends and visitors. We all must find our own individual ways of charting our journeys through the valleys, the plains *and* the deserts.

Following are a few quotes from my journal of the past year from my own "homeland." I have commented briefly on how I interpreted what I wrote and what my writing showed me about my own blind spots and unreflected moments. These notes to myself are an essential part of the harmony I attempt to create in my life. I cannot imagine the Bruch violin concerto without the throbbing base line of cello which moves in answer and question and again in response to the central theme of the violin. It is the heartbeat of the concerto, it gives it life, rhythm, density and calls it into being. My journal provides me with the same thrum of accompaniment as Bruch's base line. It is the heartbeat that tells me I am alive, it is the response that allows me to ask the next question. I would not want to play solo without it, without my notes to myself.

Entry — Summer 1995

"The roses are a disaster—burnt and beetled before they open. They have gone straight from the cradle to the grave—no coy mistress in my garden—no template for Shakespeare, Donne, or Marlowe to use in cautionary ode against wasting the time of full bloom which is so short lived. It is sad. There is a sense of failure, impotence and asexuality in a garden that does not bloom."

When I wrote this I was very discouraged about the failure of my newly planted and much anticipated roses to come to bloom. I was going through a period of disappointment with myself, feeling that nothing in my life was working as I had planned. I was physically exhausted and sick from, as yet undiagnosed, Epstein-Barr virus and attempting to lead a normally full life in a state of utter depletion. And I was fighting all the way. There was no surrender in me at all to things as they were. The result was I saw death and attrition everywhere. I saw and wrote about what was symbolic of my state of mind.

Entry—

"Another brutal day of heat. It is heat which is suffocating, it creates its own architecture of claustrophobia which is encasing me, no way out. A dark pall hangs over everything, neither the pool nor the beach escapes its shroud. This is weather that could drive one to murder or mayhem. I am exhausted from another night up at 4:00 A.M. with Patou (my dog). I did not feel like St. John of the Cross walking love-struck in the darkness, alight with his passion. My thoughts, far from love's radiance, were that Patou is an insufferable ball breaker. But I was so awake I decided to look up those lovely opening lines of St. John's 'Dark Night of the soul.'"

"On a dark night, kindled in love with yearning
Oh happy chance!
I went forth without being observed, My house
Being now at rest."

My house was definitely not at rest, not the house of my soul nor the house of my dog and I. I am quite sure St. John was not, in the inspired moment in which he wrote those lines, living with a Havanese puppy.

Entry —

"The storm caused the lights to flicker on and off all night, and there were four short outages. Somehow I managed to stay in 'eternal time,' take myself out of the angst of losing electricity and think, in the grand scheme of things, what the hell. It was more composure of desperation than of peace and surrender. I am either entering a new level of acceptance or have reached an advanced state of 'je m'enfoutism'—I tend to think the latter. I am feeling unusually calm, but it may be the extreme end line of disinterest."

The summer actually had brought me to a different level of acceptance than I had previously been capable of. As always a lesson learned *through*, not *around*, pain and alienation. But I could not give myself credit for growing, instead I chalked it up to the desperation of fatigue and boredom.

As I began to come back to myself my journal reflected another perception. I started seeing the things I care about again. The claustrophobia and disorientation began to lift, and Lazarus-like, I began to live again. It shows in what I chose to write about.

Entry —

"I accidentally got up at six instead of seven this morning. I suppose I now need glasses to get out of bed—how depressing. After initial irritation I gave into

the advantages of an early morning. The hand of God
manifests itself in these hours. The sky was a Tiepolo
ceiling. It would not have struck me as strange to see
cherubim and seraphim perched in the pink and gray
mottled clouds which swirled around the sun. Its rays
splayed out from the heavens like the fingers of God in
the Adam painting in the Cistine Chapel. Aside from that
moment of glory, I also got the laundry done. Perhaps
there are hidden advantages to nearsightedness after all."

This moment of perception was the beginning of my return from
the abyss, my journey back out of the desert. It had been a
summer of tremendous separation from self and the world. Depression is lack of connection, it is being removed from all reaction and interaction with one's self and their surroundings. It
is the complete fall from that state of grace which Anne Morrow
Lindbergh describes as being paramount to life. The desert is a
necessary part of the itinerary—we need this part of the un-
mapped territory, these states of emptiness in order to see freshly
again and be filled again, renewed in change.

But deserts are always a trial. They are meant to be. Long ago,
before the days of oil discovery, the desert fathers went into the
desert wilderness for solitude and challenge. They went there to
find their God and themselves. Pierre Tailhard de Chardin wrote
of the desert experience in *The Heart of the Matter*:

"The man was walking in the desert, followed
by his companion, when the thing swooped down on
him . . .
"The hurricane was within himself.
"And now, in the very depths of the being it invaded,
the tempest of life, infinitely gentle, infinitely brutal, was
murmuring to the one secret point in the soul which it
had not demolished. "You called me: here I am. Driven

*by the Spirit far from humanity's caravan routes, you
dared venture into the untouched wilderness; grown weary
of abstractions, of attenuations, of the wordiness of social
life, you wanted to pit yourself against reality entire and
untamed.*

*"You had need of me in order to grow; and I was
waiting for you in order to be made holy.....I am the
fire that consumes and the water that overthrows. I am
the love that initiates and the truth that passes away. All
that compels acceptance and all that brings renewal; all
that breaks apart and all that binds together; power,
experiment, progress-matter: all this am I."*

We have always sought these confrontations in the desert that
leave us transformed. Now the actual deserts are filled with oil
rigs and warfare, and the whir of angels' wings is blurred in the
churn of modern life. Deserts have become metaphors for those
moments of aloneness and absence we pass through on the way
to the next step. They are still the uncharted wastelands which
we must make part of our map. They still exist, within our souls,
and the joy of renewal when one comes out of the desert re-
deems the discomforts of going through it.

I know when I start seeing Tiepolo skies and the hand of God
in the morning clouds that I have once more come out of the
desert of my depression. My writing changes, I see connecting
links again and make new associations. Writing allows me to
become part of my habitat, both external and internal. Without
a journal in progress I feel lost, as if vital guidelines were missing.

I have picked random jottings from my last year's journal to
give an indication of the varied subjects that "speak" to me and
have a relevance in my day, no matter how fleeting or inconsequential. I find that if something draws my attention there is
a reason for it, not necessarily one that I will recognize at the
moment, but the relevance does come.

Anne Lamott's, "determined writing philosophy" is "If you get what is inside of you out it can save you, and if you don't get it out it can kill you." This year, like all the years in which I have kept journals, would not have truly belonged to me or become a part of me if I had no record of it. Going back over it gives me a feeling that I am complete, not just an ongoing series of unconnected actions and events. I can see *me*, the person, in my writing. It is an essential reality check. It is easy to disappear, and my journal keeps that from happening. Much of what I write about may appear of little consequence, but usually the entries have come into being for some reason. Like Boudin I am fascinated, and perhaps too much influenced, by weather, and it is often the beginning of my day's entry. There is a Spanish saying *cada loca su tema*, each lunatic has his theme. Well, weather is one of mine, bear with me.

December

*"Heavy silent snowfall—my small domain looks
like a child's toy globe righted after being turned upside
down, snow falling in slow motion onto the minute world
below it. Weather predictions are ominous, and the
possibility of an electrical outage looms with frightening
possibility. The lily pond looks medieval and monastic,
Bacchus is now covered to his neck and St. Francis
buried to the cupped bird held to his chest. Between them
only the upraised trumpet of the angel shows—is it an
indication that I can still be heard? The stone guard
dogs by the front door look like Ventian Doges in their
helmeted caps of white. There are two articles in the
New York Times which make me think the outside
world is still balanced. A concert pianist hauled his
Steinway to the top of an isolated cliff canyon and*

plays Chopin under the moon and stars to a few native
Americans in the valley below. He plays at sunrise and
sunset, and Chopin echoes where only they and God can
hear his music. Also reassuring is a French strike for the
right of all office workers to have a window in their
place of work so they can gauge the sun's passage in
their otherwise mechanically clocked days. Sanity will
prevail! Lilco did not fail, and I walked Patou at night
reassured by porch lights. She has the heart and soul of
a husky on a mission and bounds in snow up to her
haunches, snow bearded face smiling in delight. The
ground lamps are sunk in snow pockets and glow like
small spaceships from another planet.

"The brilliant December sun casts long attenuated
shadows, and skeletal bushes form reflections. The beach
is empty and pristine, waves break in a soft curl and the
ocean is steely, 3:00 P.M. light is celestially radiant.
The sky has a washed out and clouded brilliance, almost
colorless, but intense. A December, shortest daylight of the
year, sky. Winter chores are more time consuming than
summer's. Cinderella at the fireplace and Renfrew of the
Mounties outside. Put on Sherman-tank snow tires so I
can be liberated and cabin fever released. Waiting at
Citgo with nothing to do I looked at the Christmas
Cards taped to the walls and found myself feeling I was
in their rustic and Brueglian scenes of tree carting and
village Christmas ritual—it was like taking a vacation. I
need to stop and do nothing more often and drift into my
imagination—it will take you anywhere. Now with six
bags of kitty litter in the trunk and Mac truck tires I feel
like Romulo—invincible!

"My life is flying apart into the 'thousand and one
things,' the time consuming and frustrating maintenance
and repair efforts of the post-Newtonian mechanistic era.
The only way to write is to live in a log cabin, sans
chien and sans machines. The sky, driving home, had an

*iridescent lucidity and light reflected from the sun
pinkened the snow, it made me wonder how life can ever
become so stupidly complicated. There were hundreds of
geese flying high and wildly out of their usual grand
pattern of V's, more like starlings in their fall frenzy
than geese. The arrow patterns were fluid in their
movement, painting the sky in their design like slinkies in
a free fall, filling the air with their honking. They looked
compassless, bereft victims of a deep amnesia of where
they were supposed to be going. Are they too victims of
the machine age?"*

J a n u a r y

*"Back to writing after Christmas and New
Years and weather. I had almost forgotten how much
work it is, how much concentration is involved. It is easy
for me to let words take over content, let them become
exhibitionistic rather then conveyers of meaning. I get
carried away in my own mythologies, metaphysics and
metaphors. I have to be careful not to do an Umberto
Ecco 'look at my brilliance' distortion of what is
important in my besottment with language and the word.*

*"The deck under a full moon, sahara-duned in snow,
looks like a dimly lit stage—set for what? The big
question of the New Year!*

*"Recycling was a Hitchcockian nightmare: gulls
circling in dive bomber squads, the 'mentally challenged'
amongst them squatting in the parking area like rebellious
settlers refusing to abandon their stakes. I almost ran one
over, which I'm sure would have triggered off an animal
rights lunatic dumping their in vino veritas green glass
bottles. Luckily I missed!*

"It is too cold to walk. A January down mood has

hit, and I am waiting to want again. Desire is all, one
acts by rote without it. This is a forced amnesty, but the
rewards of surrender are usually the same; forced or
voluntary, it is a prerequisite for receiving. I feel that I
have not made great use of these snowbound days, but I
also feel like a survivor and stronger, more myself for
reasons I cannot identify anymore than I can identify
faith. Small things: I remembered to keep the front glass
door open so I could shovel a kiddy size pee patch for
Patou. Cabin fever mounted along with the escalating six
foot mound of snow at the end of the driveway on the
day I got plowed out. We are never pushed beyond our
limits—right to the bloody brink, but not beyond!

"I watched one and a half hours of Pride and
Prejudice on TV. It's a debasing medium, no wonder I
never watch it. Jane Austen affects me with longing for
the married state in spite of her obvious hints that it is
not necessarily the blessed condition we may like to think
it is. I long for a Sense and Sensibility Colonel
Brandon, even knowing that we would only be able to
tolerate each other for 24 hours at best before the hatchets
came out. I have not identified the root cause, but the
longing is there. Perhaps that is as much a part of
January as cabin fever. No Colonel Brandon's around
here, so no fear that I might succumb to a seasonal
aberration of yearning!"

"If one believes that God is, then just being is total
completion. Yet just being is the hardest thing we are
asked to do. It's so simple, we do not have to be more
than we are meant to be—but the complicated and
devious ways in which we work our way through the
grand scheme are truly amazing. One plus in my life
which is probably age related (thank God some things
still weigh in on the plus side of the balance) is a sense
of fearlessness. It is a free floating lack of fear which is
based on the feeling that I will not suffer loss or the
angst of abandonment—which has always been the
lurking dark side of happy moments.

"*The government is grinding its way to a dead halt
and the president is off on the evils of defenestration!
Husbands do not throw your wives out of windows. I
think we can all figure out the morality of that one,
what takes some doing is figuring out how to eat when
the paychecks stop. Steve Forbes is right out of the demon
pages of the DSMR III [the diagnostic manual of mental
illness]—affectless, a guy who could go on a mayhem
massacre.*

"*Woke to one of those inexplicable moods which are
always the gift of a regained self. A feeling of protection
from evils unknown and an anticipation of things to
come. It is a sense of self so profound it has nothing to
do with new clothes, new jewelry, new lovers, but
everything to do with the possibility of a renewed and
refreshed soul. There is redemption even in January!*

"*I watched the ballroom dancing competition on TV—
fabulous dancing, I had forgotten how beautifully man
and woman can move together. It's nice to see men acting
like men, flinging their partners around in dips and
swirls, in absolute male dominance. You could cut the
feeling of sex with a knife! The dance floor seems to have
escaped feminist neutering, they must be tearing their hair
out if they tuned in for this demonstration of all they
most malign. On the other hand, as great as it is on the
dance floor and in the bedroom, this male macho is not
what one wants in the kitchen or when one's feeling sick
and the kids' carpool is waiting.*"

February 14—

"*Trees are Dübreresque and grimly dead of
winter. A kamikaze spirit is needed these days to get on
the road, but death by cabin fever is worse. I've been*

flattened by exhaustion and take narcoleptic naps in the
afternoon. So much of perception is the energy one brings
to seeing, exhaustion depletes vision. Salome's veils lie
heavy on the real world in winter, but they do lift in
glorious moments to reveal wonders. A full moon rose
through the remains of sunset clouds, brilliant pink as it
rose, whitening little by little as it lost the cast of the
setting sun. I may never see a pink full moon again. One
of those miracles of the moment. Minor expectation
unfulfilled is like opening the lid of a box and finding a
black and empty hole. I bought myself three stems of
peach colored roses in an attempt to fill the black hole of
a lonely Valentine's day—it worked!

"This morning at 7:00 A.M. the whole world was
covered in hoarfrost, gray and grayish green. I felt I was
in a Hollywood setting for a horror movie on Mars. It
took me awhile to feel remotely optimistic about this day.
Later the winter fields showed some gold amidst the white
snow, clouds blew in finger-painted formations and the
wind turned the snowy road into a desert of imaginary
sand. The 'Caucasian Suite' was playing on public radio
and I felt I was out on the steppes. Thank God for a
vivid imagination when one leads a confined and
repetitive life. It takes me on the best journeys. This place
is so beautiful when it is not all summer hyped up and
soulless. It's worth the winter weather.

"Patience has its rewards—the amaryllis I bought in
October and thought defective, keeping it only as an act
of faith, has finally bloomed, one enormous blossom of
light defusing brilliant pink. God's timing is not to be
thrown away.

"Lunch at Ferriére during a brief New York jaunt. I
know why I miss France—it's so much fun to watch
people. The usual 'Euro-trash' on display faded into
blandness on the entrance of a flamboyant woman well
beyond "une certaine age:" faded blond ponytail caught

up in rhinestones, silver studded motorcycle boots, and
low-cut, black, bra revealing, blouse tucked into bulging
black satin 'jeans.' She nipped into her salade niçoise
gesticulating wildly with that animal gusto we Americans
find so unseemly. This enthusiasm for things of the flesh
has always seemed to imply a wonderfully abandoned
sexuality in the bedroom. But who knows, she may be
over the hill in that department as well. She certainly did
manage to cast a sexual mantle over the place for her
brief moment, a feat of magic absent from this long,
dreary country winter."

March

"The lily pond has unfrozen, and some of the
goldfish have come to life again. Their golden orange
bodies slowly cruise the black water. Three floated
bleached and bloated, wild eyed in their frozen death and
I lacrosse chucked them into the woods.

"Translucent light filters in through the blinds at a
new angle, and I am getting up at 6:30. The hours
before 8:00 seem to have more than the sixty minutes of
the rest of the day. They are in slow time, the rush of
the day to follow. The geese are back, their brown and
black bodies blend into the spring-waiting brown fields.
The big houses are undergoing a reverse-Christo
unwrapping of their canvas protected trees and bushes.
There is a new beige blush softening the harsh skeletal
outlines of bush and limb. The bright green crocuses look
orphaned in their casings of brown mud and dead leaves.
It stays light until 6:00.

"Mathew Fox wrote, 'We were put on this earth to
learn about love.' Compassion is perhaps the real face of
'charity.' It is the side of love I have not equated with

'love,' i.e. sex, ego and illusion. Compassion is the
connecting link. I do not have to be perfect, but I do
have to connect. Old yearnings and associations die
hard, though, and I feel an emptiness in my life which is
so tangible I would paint it if I were a painter—the
dead center of a volcano, once alive in fire, now only
black coals. Ecstasy has burned out of my pleasant
chaste days. God Almighty I miss it! Compassion Anne,
remember compassion! But there are days when
'compassion doesn't cut it'—desire, ecstasy and love are
required. 'Les neiges d'antan,' [The snows of yesteryear],
have avalanched into my thoughts today in a great
sweep of 'ubi sunt,' ['where are . . .'] I must remember
that these lovely 'neiges d'antan,' which I always thought
I could innocently turn into playful snowballs, often
came crashing down on me in avalanches of disaster.
How euphoric memory can be on a bleak spring day,
how enviable the past, how tantalizing regret, how easy
to look back and wish for what I no longer have—and
how disastrous!"

April 1

" 'The cruelest month' is starting out in sleeting
rain. Gertrude Bell in her dangerous and exotic travels
felt overwhelmed in loneliness when she was, as often
happened, in places where she was unknown. We need
reflectors of ourselves—to be known—to be identified.
This is why we write and go to psychotherapists and
need connecting links with mankind.

"I feel like a ghost. I am disappearing, failing to
register in the real world. The checks I ordered months
ago are lost, ditto the lyme test I thought might explain
why I feel so awful. I seem to have gone off the map!

"Patou is the Sarah Bernhardt of dogs. Going to the groomers, when she recognized where she was headed, her spirit of adventure did a quick volte face, *oh shit, before she went into the trembling routine. What a riot!*

"I watched the Met's Easter opera on TV. I couldn't understand why Cinderella *had been chosen until I was well into it. It is a story of renewal and resurrection, of redemption and ultimately of salvation. Cinderella offers the beggar, (the King's tutor), bread. Her goodness and innocence are Christ-like and will save the failing kingdom. There is an enormous amount of symbolism in it and it is as moving in its own way as* Parsifal *was a few years ago. Ceilia Bartoli was a delight and having a wonderful time. She obviously has the great good fortune—grace—to be doing what she loves. No lines of confusion about who she was meant to be and who she is becoming. Which means, of course, that she is very good at what she does."*

Easter

"I dyed red eggs for lunch. What a mess. I wound up with the hennaed hands of an Arab bride and Patou has a pink beard from putting her face in the egg basket. At lunch, vis-à-vis an Easter-inspired conversation I tried to explain that for me it's not 'the mystery' that presents problems—it's so called 'reality' that's the crunch. Hard to explain, harder to understand if one does not know 'the mystery.' Everyone loved cracking the pink-red eggs against each other à la Greek Easter tradition.

" 'Cruelest month' is an understatement! There are inches of fucking snow again. It's heavy wet spring snow, I suppose beautiful to eyes not blind to winter

*wonderlands which mine certainly are by now. Snow
sticks to everything. The evergreens are heavily weighted,
dragging like a nine months pregnant mother to be.
Blazing manorial fire and blazing foul mood as I
psyched myself into more shoveling of pee paths."*

*"Today there is just a hint of the caressing softness
due us this time of year. Buds sprout on everything—
how do they know, how do they dare in the face of
endless winter weather? Brittle winter clouds are beginning
to fill with the fullness of summer. One must believe it
will happen, that Divine Order is still in place. The
parking lot is full already and it's not even May—bodes
ill for the summer. I can feel the seizures of
claustrophobia starting—and anger, which is always a
disaster. Surrender to things as they are (not as I want
them to be) is not my forté. The beach is in turmoil:
sand blown into the parking lot in desert dune waves,
white slashed ocean roiled into chaotic breakers. How can
anyone look at this and still maintain the fiction that he
or she is in control?"*

*"Julian Barnes quotes Flaubert as writing, 'And was
it in any case a necessary truth: in order to be a writer
you needed to decline life?' Good question. I find myself
wanting to decline what many people seem to claim is
'life' most of the time. But I am also beginning to feel
happy in my new, middle-years skin, my evolving
persona, and I am now often able to honestly say, 'Je
suis bien dans ma peau!' [loosely translated: 'I feel
comfortable in my own skin'] (do Americans not use this
expression because we seldom feel 'well in our skins'?)—
Worth all the declining necessary to get there."*

*"According to the Atlantic Monthly Venus is the
brightest it will be for a century. It lies just north of the*

*new moon and is so brilliant it is as if no other star
exists in the heavens. The swan is back in main pond
after her winter vacation who knows where. She lay like
a white python, neck serpentined into her body at the
side of the water."*

May

*"I finished the review and like it. I love writing
because, among other things, it has a life of its own, an
extension of myself which constantly surprises me with
who I really am."*

*"This morning the kitchen window streamed tears.
Enormous pear shaped tragic droplets fell in straight lines,
prison barring the glass against another gray and sun
abandoned day. I have no desire to go out in this
ongoing onslaught of foul weather, I feel like a prisoner.
Later the sun attempted to break through the gloom and I
took a walk on the beach to reaffirm why I live here. A
heavy vehicle had castled the sand into a miniature
medieval walled fortress. Thank God for fantasy, and
those slowed down moments when images do not
disappear in speed and imagination can fly free to, as
Kundera writes, 'gaze into god's windows.' When kitchen
windows weep tears its time for a good look into God's."*

*"Spring did not come this year. Bloom and doom
marched along day after cold day. Winter is bearable
because there is hope of spring. When there is no spring
and a frantic summer waiting—then what? The day
started gray and purgatorial, then like Dante's journey
lightened its way into paradise, only to fall back into the
inferno by 11:00 P.M. in a diabolical storm. The entire
'Commedia' in less than twenty-four hours."*

"Throwing away versus accumulating a Collier brothers protective mess. I think people who have not dared self-explore and journey have a hard time getting rid of the past because they are scared of the future. Their security lies in the material that allows them to believe they 'exist.' Those who hang onto their paper selves are often without faith, scared of the naked present, fearful of the dark chaos beyond the parameters of their control. Ergo: 1) The journey is only possible for those who dare lose the past and the liens of known security; 2) To shed, grow, change and journey requires faith or it is unbearable."

"The possibility of publication has pushed me into instantaneous gratification overdrive. I want the book out tomorrow and the novel accepted the next day. I have to remember that all true creative acts happen in their own time and way. If I do not enjoy 'the process' and become more of who I really am in it, then my work will not be real, and it will be worthless. I cannot do unless I am, and it is in the working out of creation that we become. 'Divine Order Anne!' J. said to me yesterday, 'All artists always want more.' Il Prezzo!" [The Price!]

May 21

"90°. Jolted into full summer after a spring of perpetual rain. I walked on the beach where the tang of sea cold arrowed through the heat. The surf unfurled and beat a cavalry charge on the wind-hardened sand. I walked as close to the wet spume markings as possible jumping back when a larger wave marked the slow advance of filling tide. The jumps made me feel like a kid— fun, I need to play more often! There was a wooden

marker on the beach and someone had draped their white
shirt over it, the arms like a paschal drape of mourning
on Easter's empty cross. A reminder of redemption on a
redemptive day. A slight crescent moon sortied briefly
from behind ominous black clouds. Venus has sunk very
low, but is still brilliant.

"I feel as if my life is coming together. It is liberating
to be led back into one's original casting, to feel the edges
of the mold and know what is true. I am so lucky that
my work is also my passion. On the Feast of Pentacost,
the Holy Spirit breathed language into the apostles—how
can we let this great gift slide into oblivion? Language,
word, articulation, they are so marvelous—such fun.
The chestnuts are out by the lake, their blossoms rising in
phallic beauty like small candle flames—summer
Christmas trees."

June

"It is another world outside the N.Y.C.
parameter. The speed cycle dissolves and time comes back
into its natural rhythms. I spent all Saturday afternoon
with Olivia sitting beside a still lake doing nothing. She
does not require looking after, just admiration, I had no
book, no correcting work, just a chance to be in normal
time. Dogs swam in unleashed fraternity—an enormous
Newfoundland, hair on end, brow ruffled, stood up to his
shoulders in cold water, as close as he could get to his
genetic home. The lake looked like an impressionist
painting in its patterns of moving, dappled light,
mesmerizing in its slight shimmering changes. Looking at
Olivia, pulling down her slightly too small bathing suit
over her three year old derriére I thought, I don't want
her to be hurt, not ever, not in any way. Which is the

*way I felt about my own children. The vulnerability of
love honed in on my heart with the accuracy of Cupid's
arrow—flash, dead center hit. Of course she will know
hurt, as my children have, as I have, as all of us have.
It is what makes love such a tremendous undertaking,
and accepting the hit of Cupid's arrow the bravest act
man ever undertakes. In the quiet of an afternoon's
descent into evening I felt all NY tension release like a
slinky in an open roll down a flight of stairs."*

*"Home and back to the altered time of too much I
think I must do. Fighting time is the worst way of living
with it. I know that, and I still let the frenzy take hold.
Head and heart do not seem to be connected. When I
write time settles itself, like reading a detective story I
want to know what is going to happen, it is utterly
compelling.*

"The last paragraph of Snow Falling on Cedars
*nails it: 'Ishmail gave himself to the writing of it, and as
he did so he understood this too, that accident ruled every
corner of the universe except the chamber of the human
heart.' In writing I touch my heart, I know what is true,
that there are no accidents in my life, and time slows
because what is happening is right, for now, for me.
Without writing how would I ever know? I wouldn't."*

*"Fog and gloom again—one needs a machete to break
through to a view of the firmament and heavens above.*

*"The idea of the unicorn book came together in a flash
this morning. This week's inertia may have been a
nurturing black womb, although I had no idea anything
was germinating—the* volte face *of creative swing
again. I must learn to trust the black moods as being
part of the whole, painful as they are. Wrote for two
hours then took a break down to the beach to watch soft
waves curl onto spotless sand and a gray blue line of fog*

leave its mark of eternity on the horizon. These deserted
beach days are always a reminder of why I live here.
There is a heavy summer look to nature—sex rampant
wherever one looks, all of nature either priapically erected
or O'Keefe womb-like. Days like this I wonder how
people stay on their feet. It's a day that seems to echo
Julian of Norwich's refrain 'and all manner of thing
shall be well' quoted word for word by Eliot in 'Little
Gidding.' This rich thickness of summer enfolds me.
Summer is for fantasy and imagination, for re-creating
one's mysteries, for finding a lover and rediscovering the
sensual side of self. It is for going inside. It is for being
completed.

"Patou's shaved and tonsured head from the tick bite
infection looks awful, but love only augments with pity
and compassion."

"I feel like a puzzle made by a lunatic, chopped into
such fragmented pieces it's impossible to assemble. Another
Noah's deluge. At least I sorted out and nailed up the
roses from the knots they'd wound themselves into. Game
plan for the rest of this week, for the summer, for the rest
of my life!—stay off the treadmill of maintenance and
repair and go for a created, rather than sabotaged day."

End of June

"Pre-dark twilight unique to this time of year,
opaque, transcendent, before the days once more start to
shorten. There was a brush of gray against the sky as if
heaven had been spray painted. The clouds melted into
strange protean shapes afloat in their blue sky sea. They
had a furred rim etched in rainbow colors, and a ¾
moon was on the rise. The golden broom is now ash

color again - 'cueiller les rose d'aujourd hui!' (gather ye
rosebuds . . .) Which is exactly what I came home to
do, and the kitchen window sill is massed with them."

"Nothing is wasted if one writes. Last night's awful
geriatric cocktail party works in Chapter 3, just the
image I wanted. Everyone looked as if they had been put
in Dorian Grey's attic in childhood and finally released
ready for the shroud, mentally and emotionally stuck
forever in the twilight zone of childhood. At least they're
having fun, and they're not in a nursing home. Tonight
the beach grass looked like lances of an advancing
Saracen army. Also an image I can use. How lovely
writing is!
    "The weather is sunless, heaven absent murk. It's flat,
grey like a face from a prison cell, affectless, without
expression. Those are the dangerous faces, and this is
dangerous weather."

    "From Plato's Symposium:

        'Our desire for one another, to re-unite our
original nature, to make one out of two, to heal the state
of man, this is an ancient desire, implanted in us.
Separated, with one side only, like a flat fish, each of us
is but a half man, always looking for the other half . . .
Human nature was originally one, and we were a
whole, and the desire and pursuit of the whole is called
love.'

    "I miss love. I miss wholeness. But, when I am
feeling like Plato's 'flat fish,' a quick reminder of my
freedom rapidly swings the balance back in my favor. So
many of my friends seem burdened with pain-in-the-ass
family control struggles; parents, children, husbands,
lovers. I've had them all and I don't ever want to get ito

*either a controlled or controlling situation again—ever!
There is a price for the unencumbered life, but: #1) It
may be worth it; #2) It's what I have at the moment.
The missing other half is still the problem, but if it's been
like that since Plato it's hardly likely to change. I can
usually find some image to hang the threadbare remnants
of fantasy on—that will have to do for now."*

July

*"How do people live in jungle habitats where
they are constantly being pressure cooked in steamy heat.
A monsoon hit on the way to Amagansett, skies pitch
black, biblical rain and Zeus bolts of thunder and
lightning. I had to walk barefoot through the parking lot.
If I had chosen I could have splashed my way through
it in abandoned bliss, but instead I put myself into a
'God and nature are conspiring against me' mood which
I compounded in a 'fuck it' jaunt to the Post Office and
the IGA. By the time I got home soaked and foul
tempered the rain had stopped, leaving a steambath in its
wake. I could have stayed home while God did His thing
and done a million productive things if I had not been
obsessed by my own rigid timetable and agenda—Will I
ever learn?"*

*"The danger of summer is to cocoon myself in my
own small garden of Eden where lurks, ready to worm its
way into my life, the serpent of selfishness. Then I lose
my sense of place in the universe which is a disaster. It's
between the devil and the deep blue—outside of Eden is
intolerable in the summer. When I keep to myself too
much I, like Icharus, enter the burning wing zone. I am
trying not to let summer get to me, but it is as if the soul*

were drained out of this place for a few raucous months, replaced by spirit's polar opposites—noise, frenzy and hostility."

"A medical scare has brought me back to a much needed carpe diem, carpe momenti (seize the day, seize the moment) approach to life. In its way a very salutory focusing on the moment when the future could be dubious— which of course it always is anyway. The plus of illness is it whittles away the impediments to immediacy."

"Getting up at 6:00 had definite advantages; the mist on the tall grasses made them look as if a Venetian glass factory had worked all night in a burst of creative energy, turning them into diamanté gems. Harry Winston has nothing over this morning's burst of radiance. All is buzzing already, but nothing else has started yet so the world is just nature for an all too brief hour."

"Silence seems to have become anathema, people go to any lengths to avoid it. 'Music' ghetto beats in stores and restaurants, its thump appears on the most deserted of roads, no one seems to be able to paint a house or mow a lawn without it. Mindless music, not Bach or Vivaldi— and it is in silence that lies salvation—and contemplation, and mystery, and imaginative fantasy. Do kids fantasize anymore? How can one in a surround of synthesized thumping?"

"Patou's summer clip is so short she looks upholstered. Only her full fluffed ears hang at the side of her sweet face so she looks like Maria Theresa in Goya's portrait."

July 3 1

"Today was beyond rain into the realm of acts
of God. Mighty deluge like a glass wall of water deeper
than the hubcaps of my car in the flooded places.
Thunder and lightning like opera storm scenes.
Rigoletto on route 27. It seemed the wrath of God was
coming down on the string of beetle-eyed cars leaving
'The Hamptons' after a less than weather-blessed month.
It was frightening beyond the natural fear of dangerous
driving. It was more a primal fear that this is judgmental
weather because we have made such a royal fuck-up of
this beautiful place."

August 1

"God is definitely pissed off. Another day of
deluge for the incoming lot of trendy vacationers. Maybe
next year they'll all be so fed up they'll find another
watering hole. That would be worth all this summer's
downpours! Just to compound the whole thing, the white
birches around my house are dropping yellow leaves. Tim
says they are dying of stress. Why not? If that's the
way I feel why shouldn't they. He said, 'Here people
with money think they can do anything they want with
nature.' White birches do not belong in this zone, they
obviously hate it. I didn't put them in, but I will try to
save them. I am very attached to them and love to drive
in and see their lovely slender, swaying forms.
"The gray days and black starless nights continue as
if all signs and monstrances of God are being denied us.
I miss the lighted innuendoes of nature in this shroud of

gray. I must remember de Caussades 'Sacrament of the
Sacred Moment' when long range work projects
overwhelm me. I thought I had stopped anticipating future
problems, but it still creeps up on me occasionally.
Another mood of ou sont les neiges . . . has descended
on me remembering past summers in quiet corners of
Europe. Memories are wonderful, but at times yearnings
become overwhelming, 'les neiges d'antan' look much better
than they probably were and turn into a mountain of
snow if one lets them, a Chamonix of recall. I watched a
bit of the convention (five minutes) until I couldn't take
the Brady bunch bullshit anymore.

"This evening the sky is a Salomé's dance, veils of fog
and mist lift, then drop once more, in tantalizing shifting
layers that reveal patches of pale blue sky. On the
pebbled, un-chic inlet beach of Gardiner's bay you can
hear the lapping of the tide and churning of small stones
being worn down by millifractions in their daily jostling—
the 'sounds of silence.' It totally mitigated a day of fury
and frustration."

I have come full circle, a year's bits and pieces of my journal
writing. To end with the image of Salomé's veil is appropriate
and fitting as unveiling is exactly what journal writing does for
me. Without my journal I would have no idea of who I am
becoming. It was interesting to read over a whole year of my
life at a stretch and get an overall image of what it had been. It
was so much better than I remembered. I had forgotten fleeting
moments of great beauty, I realized I'd learned new strengths, I
can see patterns evolving. It allowed me to see myself and say,
yes, that's who I am—these are some of the signs of becoming.
In spite of how I dealt with frustration and problems it has all
worked together to be, in Julian's words, 'well.' Without this
record I would have no guide, no reminder of how very 'well'
my life is. I would be lost.

I cannot read a road map. I always get lost. I am a hopeless navigator on the road, God forbid the high seas. But I need this journal map of my life. It works for me. I understand it, it is neither mystifying, except in the sense that the deepest and love-liest parts of life are mysterious, nor is it illegible. It is the only map I use, and without it I would have no journey. I would be in perpetual shipwreck, or island marooned. Journal writing keeps me as sane as I am supposed to be. When I go back and read an entry like the one I wrote yesterday, "This morning scalloped clouds paved a pilgrim's route in the sky, the sign of Santiago marking a road to Compostela in the heavens." I know why I write on a daily basis. To find the road.

As his map was almost finished Fra Mauro wrote:

> *"I now know that the visitor I have been expecting all these years, the one in whom I have placed so much faith in providing me with the answers I so fervently sought, is none other than myself. I am my own informant, the only person capable of expressing the innate knowledge that resides in all of us. In me lies all the knowledge of the world, since it is my world alone that I wish to explore."*

These notes of mine to myself may seem trivial, bordering on the inane at times, but they are true notations of what I have been aware of in my days. That I am aware at all is always a miracle, since I, like so many people, have times of profound disconnection when nothing I "see" registers. I do not take the ability to observe for granted. Perception is a miracle, perhaps Winnicott was right and it is one of those miracles one needs to be deprived of occasionally in order to understand its quality. He claims there are benefits of wholeness in depression, that depression too is part of the entirety of man's experience. When one is in the throes of depression's disconnection it is hard to think there is any merit in such an abysmal state of psychic blindness, but I have always found that on coming out of what are mercifully short bouts of this deadened state that something was germinating. When I come back to myself it is always with renewed energy for something new, somewhere in the pits of blackness I have learned something I had to know. It usually has to do with change. Change is one of the main reasons I keep a journal, and the ability to change is one of the gifts of journal writing. I try to keep up a running inventory of directions I want to move in and old habits and reactions I am sick of and find counter-productive to the person I would like to be and feel I really am. I do not think many of us can say that everything we do and think corresponds to the way we believe ourselves to be. I do things which are so contrary to what I like to think of as my true "nature" that without reminders that this is not the way it should be, I might very well lose sight of the "nature" which is myself. My notes keep me in line with what I know to be correct, then I stand a chance of doing what is right—for me. My journal is about change, but it is also about maintenance and not losing precious ground which I have claimed for myself.

The backwards and forwards between myself and nature in the grand sense has several reasons behind it. Some of these tie in with the joy of perception and reaction and knowing it is not something I can take for granted. When I can see and describe nature I am O.K. and healthy, when I am temporarily locked into a perceptual blindness that leaves me staggering in the shadows, nature disappears from my reality. Observation of nature is my barometer, my indicator of mood, fair or foul, and it is an accurate one. I also use it as a base line for my daily notations, because I am so happy to be finally living in a place where nature is present to me. As a city girl this is still a new thrill and hopefully always will be. I like to see the analogies between the physical and mental world, and there is a vast mythology in the natural which fascinates me. I cannot think of a writer I have been attracted to who has not had his or her correspondences to nature and seen parallels and metaphorical balances between word and thing. Thomas Merton, whom I have quoted rather extensively in this text, has a way of explaining the most abstruse ideas and concepts. He manages to capture this idea of the importance of nature in the creative act, especially writing, in his book *Bread in the Wilderness:*

> *"The function of cosmic symbols in the Psalter is an important one. The revelation of god to man through nature is not the exclusive property of religion . . . Light and darkness, sun and moon, stars and planets, trees, beasts, whales, fishes and birds of the air, all these things in the world around us and the whole natural economy in which they have their place have impressed themselves upon the spirit of man in such a way that they naturally tend to mean to him much more than they mean in themselves. That is why, for example, they enter so mysteriously into the substance of our poetry, of our visions and of our dreams."*

He adds in a final and prophetic note of understanding what is behind some of the malaise of our time:

> *"That too is why an age, like the one we live in, in which cosmic symbolism has been almost forgotten and submerged under a tidal wave of trademarks, political party buttons, advertising and propaganda slogans and all the rest—is necessarily an age of mass psychosis. A world in which the poet can find practically no material in the common substance of every day life . . . can only end up, like ours, in self-destruction."*

I think we still need these basic correspondences which can only be found in the reality of nature. One of the reasons I am fascinated by the Middle Ages and Renaissance is that it was a time of allegorical thinking when man and nature were seen as reflections of each other, as part of the whole. This strong allegorical underpinning gave rise to literature that is proof of the inspiration the creative imagination can draw from a strong relationship to nature. The country keeps me sane, or helps me come back on track when I have temporarily de-railed in some self-centered mania. Like many other environmentally concerned people I hate to see the destruction and abuse of natural beauty which hacks away at ourselves at the base of our creativity and thus deprives us of an essential mirror of our souls. Finally what is outside affects profoundly what is going on inside of me, I have never learned to exclude weather from a long list of things that affect my mood. That is on the short list of things to change! For many centuries God was equated with the beautiful. God is perfect and the perfectly beautiful was considered a reflection of His goodness and being. To see beauty in nature is, to me, a God-given present, it is a glimpse of the miracle that is existence—Logically to describe the effects of nature is a way of communicating with God.

I have not included in these few quotations from my journals any of my "notes" which pertain either to family or private areas of my life. They are private and I feel should remain so. Privacy, as I discussed, is a crucial element of journal writing. They are notes to myself, as whatever you write will be notes to yourself—and you, like me, can find yourself in your pages.

I hope I have reached a few potential, if reluctant, journal writers, I hope the exercises have broken down some of the barriers to writing and the quotations have been inspiring. I have tried to find authors who have described their own search, why the journey was important to them and what they discovered as possibilities of creative self-expression and incentive to prove how seductive writing can be. For those excited about the vast possibilities open to self-exploration it will be more exciting than you can ever imagine. There is only one last word of advice and counsel, it is the word with which I started this book: Begin to map your journey and start your notes to yourself.

> *"A journey of a thousand miles must begin with a single step."*
>
> Lao-tzu

FINALE

I end this book looking backwards to the words of an eleventh century scholastic, Richard of St. Victor:

> "A man, who has not yet succeeded in seeing himself, raises his eyes in vain to see God. Let a man first understand the invisible things of himself before he presumes to stretch out to the invisible things of God . . . for unless you can understand yourself, how can you try to understand those things which are above yourself?"

ANNOTATED BIBLIOGRAPHY

Aciman, André. *Out of Egypt.* Farrar, Straus & Giroux, NY, 1994. Memoir of the author's life in Alexandria, rich in memory and nostalgia. An excellent example of why we need writing to capture and hold experience which we treasure too much to let slip away.

Alighieri, Dante. *The Divine Comedy.* Oxford University Press, NY, 1939. Translation and commentary by John S. Sinclair. A verse translation by Allen Mandelbaum, Bantam Books, 1982. Both of these translations are excellent. Their texts are accompanied by general introductions, individual canto introductions and notes to each canto. In both the translation page faces the original Italian. The notes in the Mandelbaum version are somewhat more scholarly and extensive. Although I like the idea of his verse translation I prefer the language of Sinclair. Both are available in paperback.

Allende, Isabel. *Paula,* Harper and Collins, NY, 1995. The author writes of the illness and death of her daughter and how it devastated her. A sad and beautiful example of a need to write out the horrors and agonies which are sometimes forced into our lives.

Aurelius, Marcus. *Meditations*, Penguin Books, NY, 1964. Both meditation and memoir, this small book by a Roman emperor is an indicator that man's pursuit of self-knowledge is an ageless part of the human condition and the creative act of writing a timeless way in which we find ourselves.

Boethius. *Tractates, the Consolation of Philosophy*, Harvard University Press, Cambridge, 1973. This is a book which has had great historical significance and is as relevant and readable now as it was in the 6th century. In the desperate confinement of prison Boethius uses his journal as both expiation and salvation. His writing is lucid, heartfelt and his discoveries are true epiphanies.

Bradlee, Ben. *A Good Life, Newspapering and Other Adventures*, Simon & Schuster, NY, 1995. Anyone who has ever heard or met Ben Bradlee knows how infectious his enthusiasm for life is and that enthusiasm is manifest in this interesting and open book of memoir. He gives the reader great insights into the worlds of politics and newspapers.

Breathnack, Sarah Ban. *Simple Abundance: A Daybook of Comfort and Joy*, Warner Books Inc., NY, 1995. This book has been very successful and popular as a daily self-help meditation aide. It stresses the beauty and inspirational moments of everyday life.

Caussade, Jean-Pierre de. *The Sacrament of the Present Moment*, Harper, San Francisco, 1989. The title says it all. The book is a lovely meditation on how to stay "in the now" and avoid the frenzy of past and future preoccupations.

Cowan, James. *A Mapmaker's Dream*, Shambalhala Publications Inc., Boston, 1996. A lovely poetic conversation between a monk and himself as he explores the world vicariously through other people, travelers who are not, like him, confined to a monastic cell.

Descartes, René. *Discourse and Method and the Meditations*, Sutcliffe, Penguin Books, New York, 1968. Translation F. E. Sutcliffe, Meditations on how man can know himself from a transitional moment in history.

Duchin, Peter. *Ghost of a Chance a Memoir*, Random House, NY, 1996. A fun and anecdotal book about identity. It is interesting to read about Duchin exploring self-exploration.

Eliot, T. S. *The Complete Poems and Plays 1909-1950*, Harcourt Brace Jovanovich, New York. The best edition of Eliot I know of. It includes an index of first lines which is useful and the print is legibly large. Eliot is one of my standard reference books on the bookcase next to my desk. At every reading another shade of Eliot's meaning is revealed.

Fox, Mathew. *Meditations with Meister Eckhart*, Beer & Co., Santa Fe, New Mexico, 1983. A large-print edition of some of the writings of the master who so influenced writers such as Anne Morrow Lindbergh and Dag Hammarskjöld.

Frank, Anne. *The Diary of a Young Girl*, Bantam Books, NY, 1993. A girl's diary written with humor and disingenuous honesty which is written proof of the merits, benefits and bottom line necessity of writing when one is living under extreme duress. It is a poignant, sad and funny journal, a great example of this genre.

Hammarskjöld, Dag. *Markings*, Ballantine Books, NY, 1956. Meditation, philosophy and journal all weave into each other in this small, deeply concentrated book of a well-known public figure whose private life was an enigma.

Harrison, Barbara Grizzuti. *An Accidental Autobiography*, Houghton Mifflin Co., Boston, 1996. A highly idiosyncratic medley of thoughts, travels and life experiences described by a writer who obviously has to write her life as well as live it.

Hays, David and Daniel Hays. *My Old Man and the Sea: A Father and Son Sail Around Cape Horn*, Harper Perennial, Harper Collins, NY, 1995. This book combines the journals of father and son to weave a story which proves that one version of events is never the whole picture.

Kayson, Susanna. *Girl, Interrupted*, Vintage Books, Random House Inc., NY, 1993. A tragi-comedy of confinement in a mental institution and, like Styron's book, a solid endorsement of the therapeutic benefits of journal writing.

Lamott, Anne. "Bird by Bird", *Some Instructions on Writing and Life*, Anchor Books, Doubleday, 1994. One of the best books on writing I know. Written from experience with humor and insight, and absolutely no pedantry. She makes writing a very accessible occupation and delight.

Langewiesche, William. *Sahara Unveiled*, Pantheon Books, NY, 1996. A beautiful travel narrative of the desert.

Lawrence, Lady. *Indian Embers*, Trackless Sands Press, Palo Alto, CA, 1991. This book serves two functions; it is a documentary of the end of the British Raj in India, and a writer's secret discourse with herself in the face of adjustments and hardships which came with being married to a British Officer at the time.

Lessard, Suzannah. *The Architect of Desire: Beauty and Danger in the Stanford White Family*, the Dial Press, NY, 1996. This is a beautifully written psychological portrait of a woman coming to terms with a difficult past.

Lindbergh, Anne Morrow. *Gifts from the Sea*, Vintage Books, Random House, NY, 1991. This well-known and popular book is the quintessential journal. It shows why the "examined life" is worth the effort.

Mallon, Thomas. *A Book of One's Own: People and Their Diaries*, Hungry Mind Press, Saint Paul, Minnesota, 1995. A good, generalized overview of well-known diarists.

Maslow, Abraham H. *Towards a Psychology of Being*, 2nd edition. Van Nostrand Reinhold, NY, 1968. This is a classic on the subject of man's road to self-realization and self-actualization. Maslow originated the concept of "peak experiences" and explains their nature. The text occasionally verges on the academic in its writing, but is generally quite readable.

Merton, Thomas. *The Ascent to Truth*, Harvest Book, Harcourt Brace Jovanovich, 1981. Thomas Merton must be read to experience his utterly unique ability to capture feeling, especially spiritual revelation, in word. He comes as close to being able to describe the ineffable as any writer I know.

————. *The Seven Story Mountain*, Harvest Book, 1948. Thomas Merton's autobiography, a classic example of memoir and journal coming together in the recounting of how the author discovers his path. His journals make good continuing reading.

Miner, Earl. *Japanese Poetic Diaries*, Berkeley University of California Press, 1969. An example of the highly creative potential of travel writing, where it can become in and of itself a work of art.

Norris, Kathleen. *The Cloister Walk*, Riverhead Books, NY, 1996. A writer's journal of the rewards and surprises of incorporating a monastic life into her married existence. Beautifully written, and filled with lovely quotations. One woman's search for a completed identity and an insightful look at how a writer's mind works.

Pamuk, Orhan. *The Black Book*, Harvest Book, Harcourt Brace & Co., NY, 1996. One of the most original and revealing novels about identity (how we find it, how we know it, or does it in actuality even exist?) that I have come across.

Pascal, Blaise. *Pensées*, Penguin Books, London, 1966. Translation Krailsheimer, A. J. Highly cerebral targeting of our strengths, weaknesses, heroics, and follies in the pursuit of our destinies. Filled with one-liners most of us probably never knew we knew.

Pipher, Mary. *Reviving Ophelia: Saving the Selves of Adolescent Girls*, Ballantine Books, NY, 1995. A best-selling book on why and how adolescent girls lose their sense of completeness and identity. The author explains how important the creative act, specifically journal writing, is in maintaining and relocating perception of identity. The book is written around case studies which underline the important role of creativity in establishing a unique self.

Pope John XXIII, *Days of Devotion, Daily Meditation from the Good Shepherd*, Viking, A Giniger Book Penguin Book, 1967. Daily readings of meditation drawn from the Pope's life and spiritual experience.

Saint Augustine. *Confessions*, Translation R. S. Pine Coffin, Penguin Books, NY, 1961. This memoir/journal seems contemporary in its readability. It is open and explicit in its confession and search for a "new life" of the spirit when the flesh still calls with great siren songs of appeal. These confessions probably bring the reader as close as he or she will ever come to an understanding of the struggle involved in becoming a saint.

Saint John of the Cross. *Dark Night of the Soul*, Image Books, Doubleday, NY, 1995. The mystical experience in poetry. The work contains extraordinary images.

Saint Teresa of Avila Fount. *The Interior Castle*, Harper Collins, Great Britain, 1995. This 16th century saint lived an interior life of great intensity. She was greatly involved in both political and mundane affairs and she describes this flow between the inside and outside castles of her life in lucid and poetic prose.

Scott, Robert Falcon. *Scott's Last Expedition, The Journals*, Carroll & Graf Inc., NY, 1996. A meticulously kept journal of the outward and inward bound journey of this doomed polar expedition.

Scott-Maxwell, Florida. *The Measure of My Days*, Borzoi Books, Alfred A. Knopf, NY, 1968. What can happen when a writer in her eighties describes the changes that are still taking place in her evolving persona.

Shakespeare, William. *The Riverside Shakespeare*, Houghton Mifflin Company, Boston, 1974. The standard student text for Shakespeare with excellent general introduction and particular introductions to each play and section. All introductions and textual notes well written and highly informative. Typesetting small but readable.

Shirer, William. *Berlin Diary: The Journal of a Foreign Correspondent 1934-1941*, Little, Brown and Company, 1940. A mixture of political and personal commentary which gives the reader insight into a world in transition (for the worse).

Styron, William. *Darkness Visible: A Memoir of Madness*, Vintage Books, Random House Inc., NY, 1992. A classic in the annals of writing about the devastation of depression. The book is short, lucid and brutal, and proof positive of the therapeutic benefit of journal writing under duress.

Teilhard de Chardin, Pierre. *The Heart of the Matter*, Harvest Book, Harcourt Brace Jovanovich NY., 1976. An at times controversial Catholic priest-cum-paleoanthropologist describes his thoughts on, and search for, "the heart of the matter."

Trilling, Diana, *The Beginning of the Journey: The Marriage of Diana and Lionel Trilling*, Harvest Book, Harcourt Brace & Company, NY, 1993. This is an interesting use of memoir to set the record straight on two lives whose public version did not always coincide with what the author knew to be the truth.

Winnicott, D. W. *Home is Where We Start From: Essays by a Psychoanalyst*, W. W. Norton & Co., NY, 1990. A psychoanalyst's viewpoint of creativity and how creative acts affect the human psyche. Easily accessible to the lay reader.